Praise for
Redesign Your Mind

"Eric Maisel is at the cutting edge in the field of creativity and health. I've used the practices and exercises described in *Redesign Your Mind* myself and they really work! Plus, they are fun to read and easy to use. I highly recommend this must-read book."

—**Jed Diamond,** PhD, author of *The Enlightened Marriage*

"Once again, Eric Maisel has translated complex ideas into everyday language. Using the visual metaphor of 'the room that is your mind,' he presents practical applications that can restore well-being in times of emotional and existential angst. Perfect for creatives and for everyone whose mind could use an upgrade."

—**Chuck Ruby,** PhD, executive director of the International Society for Ethical Psychology and Psychiatry

"Within the room that is our mind, many people spread anger, guilt, worry, and resentment. Dr. Eric Maisel teaches us how the mind has the ability to enter into self-conversation and dynamic self-regulation to change all that. The results are profound and bring expanded awareness, insight, inspiration, creativity, and focused concentration."

—**Lee Jampolsky,** PhD, bestselling author of *Healing the Addictive Personality*

"With humor and compassion, Maisel describes more than fifty exercises for trading in one's self-pestering thoughts for healthy indwelling. The book's engaging and practical tools teach readers to be gentle with themselves and achieve new heights of understanding and creativity. This book is not just inspirational; it brings profound relief."

—**Judith Schlesinger,** PhD, author of *The Insanity Hoax: Exposing the Myth of the Mad Genius*

Redesign
Your Mind

Redesign Your Mind

The Breakthrough Program
for Real Cognitive Change

Eric Maisel, PhD

CORAL GABLES

Published by Mango Publishing, a division of Mango Media Inc.

Cover Design: Jermaine Lau
Layout & Design: Jermaine Lau

For permission requests, please contact the publisher at:
Mango Publishing Group
2850 S Douglas Road, 2nd Floor
Coral Gables, FL 33134 USA
info@mango.bz

For special orders, quantity sales, course adoptions and corporate sales, please email the publisher at sales@mango.bz. For trade and wholesale sales, please contact Ingram Publisher Services at customer.service@ingramcontent.com or +1.800.509.4887.

Redesign Your Mind: The Breakthrough Program for Real Cognitive Change

Library of Congress Cataloging-in-Publication number: Pending
ISBN: (p) 978-1-64250-511-5 (e) 978-1-64250-512-2

BISAC category code: PSY045070, PSYCHOLOGY / Movements / Cognitive Behavioral Therapy (CBT)

Printed in the United States of America

TABLE OF CONTENTS

FOREWORD

As a psychologist, academic, and author for forty years, I have read my share of books designed to help in life. A few boxes must be checked to recommend a book: it must be practical and straightforward to apply, immediately applicable, innovative, not put the reader to sleep, increase peace of mind, and expand awareness. Frankly, most books fall far short. In contrast, Dr. Eric Maisel checks all the boxes with *Redesign Your Mind.*

"You are what you think." It doesn't get more straightforward than this. But sometimes simple truths become overly complicated theories, and such is the case with many books on Cognitive Behavioral Therapy (CBT). As a result, many books on CBT are, to be blunt, dull. Dr. Maisel's book is anything but boring. Additionally, although many other books describe CBT well, they read like a cookbook, far from experiencing the many facets of the actual meal. In *Redesign Your Mind,* we not only learn about cognitive psychology, but we also experience what it is like to have a mind, specifically, what it feels like to inhabit in our own mind.

Dr. Maisel is not a newbie to this subject. His decades of work have profoundly affected the thinking and quality of life of countless individuals worldwide. In his latest book, we not only get insight into how we think, we obtain skills to discover who we are and what we are here to do. This book will help you see both the problems in the way you think and the solutions, and, before you know it, you will be stepping forward with unique honesty and the ability to free yourself from old dysfunctional patterns.

For years, you may have been unknowingly busy building walls with your thoughts and imprisoning yourself behind them. By practicing the exercises in this book, you will be reaching the core of who you are in remarkable new ways and learning that amid your most significant challenges, you can become more calm, effective, and aware of your power to free yourself. You are, quite literally, about to see with renewed clarity and move beyond concepts and constructs in your mind that caused you to behave in ways that limited your happiness and success. By the end of this book, if you practice the exercises, you will discover your mind is extraordinary in what it can create.

Whenever I have a chance to talk with a fellow author, I ask them what they wish for the reader, which tells me a great deal. Dr. Maisel eloquently answered me: "The book goes deeper than just 'managing your thoughts,' it changes the very source of your thoughts—the room that is your mind—so that you no longer think thoughts that aren't serving you. You end up with a much fresher, breezier, nimbler mind." I love this answer and, after reading the book, I can tell you that Eric more than achieves his goal.

If you believe that you are just a product of the world around you—that your happiness is dependent on this thing or that person—then you are always going to be a victim of circumstance to one degree or another. One of the most liberating personal discoveries you will make is knowing that whenever you are upset, you have the power to shift your thinking and discover a peace you never knew existed. When you are unsettled, you most likely don't quickly see the real cause of your upset or the solution. This book helps you stop wasting your life wishing for a better past, blaming your present circumstances, or blindly hoping for a better future. In short, the practice of the exercises frees you to create, grow, succeed, and love.

Gerald Jampolsky, MD

INTRODUCTION

Let's get you a whole new mind, shall we?

It would be lovely if you could do a better job of dealing with all those thoughts that aren't serving you. That alone would be a really useful upgrade! But what if you could go a giant step further and stop those thoughts from even entering your mind? Wouldn't that be *the best*?

Well, you can do exactly that!

For thousands of years, philosophers have tried to describe consciousness and explain how the mind works, but we aren't going down that road. We are opting for a super-simple, super-useful model. We are going to picture your mind as a room that you inhabit. I'm inviting you to think of it as a literal place where you go to think and be. That's the metaphor we're going to use and the picture we're going to paint.

And indeed, "the room that is your mind" is the most important place in your universe! Now, probably for the first time, you get to redesign it, redecorate it, and really take charge of it. As you do, you will start thinking and feeling differently about your life. Just picture the difference between a bright, sunny room and a drab, claustrophobic room. In which one do you want to live? Wouldn't you be quite the different person if you got to leave that drab one, where you've been living *your whole life long*, and start living in that bright one? Wouldn't that make a tremendous difference in how you thought and felt? Of course, it would!

Starting right now, I'd like for you to believe that you can redesign and redecorate "the room that is your mind." Why shouldn't you be able to? You're in charge of that room, aren't you?

So what exactly are we doing? We're *visualizing* change. I want you to see that room, really picture it, and get behind making changes to it. You can decide later if this process has actually worked. The first step is to give it a try.

Here's what I'd like you to do first. Get yourself a journal or open a file on your computer dedicated to our work together. I'll be providing you with a writing prompt at the end of each chapter and I hope that you'll take the time to respond to those prompts. Here's the first one:

I've been living in "the room that is my mind" my whole life. What has that felt like?

If you took the time to write, I hope that you've already learned a little something about what living in your particular mind has felt like. Maybe you didn't really have adequate language to describe how living there has felt. That's okay. If you tried your best to capture some of your experience living in your own mind, that's great! That's all I'm asking—for you to engage with these ideas.

Let's try a second writing exercise. In a moment, I'll ask you to describe your "indwelling style." What do I mean by that? Picture a country cottage versus an ultra-modern home. Each has a different style. You can easily picture the decorations in one versus the decorations in the other. The cottage might have carved wooden picture frames, and the modern homes may have brushed steel ones. In each, everything would hang together because there was an overarching style or theme. Well, the way we inhabit the room that is our mind has its own particular style. What's yours?

Maybe you're always a little frightened and anxious in there, so you have an *anxious indwelling style*. Maybe you're very critical and self-critical—a *critical indwelling style*. Maybe you're always right on the verge of anger, or right on the verge of sadness, so you have an *angry indwelling style* or a *despondent indwelling style*. What is "your way" of being in the room that is your mind? What's your indwelling style? Take a nice amount of time and respond to this question.

Remember, the goal isn't to arrive at the right answer or perfect understanding. *The goal is to begin getting familiar with these ideas.* This may be the first time you've ever thought about the possibility of redesigning your mind. I hope that it's a little thrilling. Be easy at the start, and keep jotting down ideas as they come to you. Those will be really fertile areas to investigate!

Now that you've gotten your feet wet thinking about "the room that is your mind" and your indwelling style, let's address what exactly you'll be doing. You're going to visit the room that is your mind and *make changes*.

Not every change I suggest will apply to you or even make sense to you, so only make the changes that seem sensible to make! I ask that you at least consider each change before rejecting it. I've worked with clients as a therapist and a coach for forty years, and each change I'm suggesting has its reasons. I think you'll see the logic to every change I suggest, so please do give each one some thought!

And please, have some fun! We are doing serious work, but we can also be a little lighthearted. You will see that there's a little cheeky joy built into each of my suggestions. I want this work to feel like the equivalent of a breath of fresh air. So add your own cheekiness and joy!

Imagine wandering about in some great flea market, on the lookout for just the right do-dads for your newly redesigned mind. The steering wheel of a great ship? No, not quite. Those gorgeous brandy snifters from Vienna? Hmm, no, not quite. But those French posters from the 1940s? They might be exactly right...

First as a therapist, and for the last thirty years as a creativity coach, I've worked with creative and performing artists, scientists and engineers, academics and entrepreneurs, and other bright, imaginative clients. All have been troubled and most have ended up with some "mental disorder" label—maybe depression, bipolar, attention deficit, or generalized anxiety. *All* smart, sensitive, creative people are troubled enough to earn some mental disorder label. That's because there is a necessary connection between intelligence, sensitivity, creativity, and distress.

Being smart, sensitive, creative, *and* troubled go hand-in-hand. What can be done to help with that? Many things, but one is by far the most important—the one that you have direct control over. You can get a grip on your own mind! Philosophers from Marcus Aurelius to the Buddha have pointed this out as our top priority. Cognitive-behavioral therapy (CBT) is the modern way that this age-old message is delivered. Why is CBT so popular that it's the primary therapy provided by the United Kingdom's National Health Service? Because its central message is indubitably true: you are what you think.

However, the ways that you're invited to get a grip on your mind, whether those invitations come from Stoicism, Buddhism, or cognitive-behavioral therapy, are a bit on the dull and stodgy side. And they miss a crucial point: a major shortcoming of CBT is that it doesn't speak to what it feels like to have a mind. We don't just "have thoughts." We keenly experience what it feels like to dwell in our own mind.

Descartes pictured it as a stage where we play out our dramas. We're going to picture it as a room—one you can design and decorate exactly as you like!

The room that is your mind isn't some optional accessory to life. It is *where* and *how* human consciousness is experienced. It is all-important, and it's yours to create and design. It's really exciting to picture transforming that room into exactly the kind of place where you would want to live. When you redesign your mind, you increase your creativity, heal from past trauma, and achieve emotional well-being. You *really* change.

Come join me on this mind-changing adventure and let's have some fun!

PART I

REDESIGNING YOUR MIND

LETTING A BREEZE IN

We are not going to trouble ourselves with arcane debates about what consciousness is, where it's located, or whether the brain and the mind are exactly the same or seriously different things. We are focusing on one beautiful idea: the room that is your mind can be redesigned to serve you better.

The first thing we're going to do is get all that stuffiness out of your mindroom! (The phrase "the room that is your mind" is a bit cumbersome, so let's use "mindroom" instead.) You've been living in your mindroom forever, thinking the same thoughts, repeating the same opinions, remembering the same hurts. It's time to throw open the windows and let a cleansing breeze blow through. That breeze will clear the air of worry and despair and clear your mind of all those thoughts that aren't serving you.

In order to throw open those windows, you first need to *install* them. Let's visualize that right now. Shut your eyes and picture your mindroom. If you can't quite picture it, just picture it indistinctly. Its contours will become clearer as we proceed. For now, just "feel" it, all its stuffiness and airlessness. Now, pick a wall and install a pair of windows. Choose any sort of window you like, and have them look out onto any sort of vista you like. What windows will you choose? And what vista?

My wife and I once rented a ground-floor apartment in Paris with tall living room windows that opened onto a lovely, quiet side street. Seated at the table by those windows, eating baguettes and drinking wine, we watched the world go by. The windows installed in my mindroom are those tall French windows. What sort of windows would you like to install? Windows looking down on Broadway, with jazz playing in the background? Old-fashioned windows with screens on them, looking out onto a lake? Exotic windows looking out at sand dunes and the sea beyond? Choose yours now!

Now, throw them wide open!

If your mindroom is like most mindrooms, it is stuffy, troubling, and much too familiar. It's full of secrets that we keep from others and secrets that we keep from ourselves. It's full of intimations of our own mortality, whispers of insults not forgotten, strange, destructive urges, and ghosts of the distant past. It is anything but light and airy! Now, you get to transform that dark place into a space that is lighter and airier. With your windows thrown wide open, let all that mustiness blow away!

When you add windows to your mindroom, throw them open, and let a welcome breeze blow through, you immediately relax, reduce your anxiety, and provide a way for sadness to escape. You make life feel less stale, repetitive, and oppressive, just like that. You can picture regrets and disappointments leaving, and you can find peace without having to engage in soothing peace substitutes like endlessly surfing the Net or drinking too much alcohol. When I throw open the windows of my mindroom, I receive amazing benefits. I feel calmer and more loving, and I think more clearly. Everything changes for the better, just as life changes for the better when a cloud passes and the sun reappears.

The Buddha's advice to "get a grip on your mind" suggests work. It is certainly work that cognitive therapists are suggesting when they ask you to engage in thought stopping, thought substituting, and so on. But adding windows and opening them wide is *easy*. It's, well, a breeze!

Please take a few moments and visualize your mindroom filled with cheery light and a gentle breeze. Just be there. There's nothing to think and nothing to do. Just throw those windows open and let a breeze blow through.

I've written fifty books and I know what writing a book takes. It takes the opposite of claustrophobia. It takes airiness, a breeze, and a blue sky. It takes concentration, but while swinging in a hammock. It takes focus, but as in a sea gaze. To write well, I need the mental equivalent of a still summer afternoon with the sounds of bees buzzing and air circulating. And I can have that! All I need to do is visit my mindroom and throw open the windows.

Let's do some right thinking to go along with that new breeziness. Let's support your intention to get rid of all that stuffiness by thinking some new thoughts that will serve you. Think one of your customary unhelpful thoughts, like "I'm not very talented," or "I've wasted a lot of time in life," or "I'm feeling very sad." At the same time, picture those open windows, feel a gentle breeze blow through, and exclaim (silently or out loud), "Breeze, take this thought away!"

Watch the thought float right out the window. Follow it in your mind's eye all the way to the sea and watch it evaporate in shafts of sunlight. Can you even remember the thought that you were thinking? No! It floated off and is gone because you installed windows and gave it a way to exit.

This is your new learning. You can always visit your mindroom, indwell there peacefully, and have the thoughts that aren't serving you drift right out the windows you've installed. Thinking about playing another video game? Visit your mindroom and let that craving drift off. Feeling sad? Visit your mindroom and let that feeling float away. Those windows really are a bit of miracle. They let everything you don't need pass right out of your mindroom and dissolve into the ether.

In the next chapter, we'll get an easy chair installed in your mindroom. How nice it will be to sit in your easy chair with a lovely breeze blowing the cobwebs away! But before we leave this chapter, I want you to visit your mindroom one last time. Go there now and picture a sunny day, your windows thrown open, and a gentle breeze blowing through. Shut your eyes, be there, and relax. This is the first major change in how you indwell, without all the usual stuffiness. Be there for a while and enjoy the experience. There's no rush. Take a moment to indwell peacefully before moving on to the next chapter.

· ✦ ○ ✦ ·

Every chapter will end with a visualization and a writing prompt. I hope you'll engage with both.

Visualization: Visualize the room that is your mind. Add windows. Open those windows. Let a breeze in!

Writing Prompt: Look around your mindroom. Do you see a piece of furniture or something else that ought to be removed? What is it and why should you get rid of it?

ADDING AN EASY CHAIR

I hope you're getting comfortable with our metaphor of "the room that is your mind," or as we're now calling it, your mindroom. That is *such* an interesting place, in part because it is where our human nature plays itself out. We do not come into the world a blank slate. We come into the world human, with instincts, proclivities, orientations, potentialities, and everything else that's part of our original nature or personality.

Think for a moment about how your original nature or personality might manifest as you go about redesigning your mindroom: how might it get in the way?

You install windows, open them, and let in a breeze. But what if your original nature finds that uncomfortable, maybe because of some archaic fear of open windows? So some force that you can't see or reckon with suddenly closes those windows. You enter your mindroom, throw open the windows, and they suddenly slam shut again! Isn't that going to feel really strange?

Ghosts. Poltergeists. I think you can sense how dynamic and fundamentally strange your mindroom is—and how fundamentally strange human nature is—because *how we intend to live* must battle the *unseen demands of our original nature*. Freud used the word "id" to describe these unseen forces, these primitive parts, these genetic deep recesses of the species. Jung used phrases like "the collective unconscious" and ideas like "archetypes" to communicate the same fundamental notion. While we'd love to redesign our minds to suit our intentions, we are bound to be partially thwarted by the strange demands of our original nature. So we have to live with this dynamic tension and *stay aware of it*.

There is nothing to be done about the fact that we come into the world with instincts, desires, and all the rest. When a window that we just opened suddenly slams shut, let's not act too puzzled or react too dramatically. Our mindroom is that sort of place: more like a haunted house than a stately library. If we are aware of that, we can live with that—and reopen the window!

Next, let's deal with the amazing self-unfriendliness that so many people display toward themselves. What's a partial solution to that? Getting rid of that bed of nails square in the center of your mindroom and replacing it with an easy chair!

I bet that right now, there is a pain-inducing bed of nails prominently positioned in the middle of your mindroom. It's the one you've installed to remind yourself *at all times* that you've failed yourself. It's there to punish you for mangling your life. Isn't part of you certain that you deserve that bed of nails, that you should writhe in pain, and that piercing yourself on those sharp metal points is the only way to expiate your guilt?

Let's get rid of it! *Right now*, visualize getting rid of it. Call in the haulers and get it the heck out. Watch the haulers leave with it. Pay them a little extra to destroy it, so that no one finds it and thinks they deserve it. Tip the haulers handsomely and thank them profusely. They are carrying out the thing that has harmed you the most: your enduring self-indictment. It is time to sign your pardon. That bed of nails is, and has always been, a cruel and unusual punishment.

Okay, it's been hauled away! Next, go online in your mind's eye and buy yourself the exact easy chair you've never permitted yourself to get. Make sure it's comfortable! Skip that chair-as-art that was never meant to be sat on. Get something comfy. You want an easy chair that is genuinely easy to relax in because that ease is going to translate into better living. Take your time shopping!

Picture where you'll place your easy chair in your mindroom. Maybe right beside one of those windows you installed! But which one: the one facing that gorgeous view, or the one that lets in the most air? Or maybe you'll put it right next to the handy small refrigerator (if impulse snacking isn't a problem for you). Get its placement pictured, make your purchase, and wait expectantly at the door when it's due to arrive.

Point the movers to exactly where you want it positioned. Then sit! Do you deserve that easy chair? Of course, you do. Do you deserve it even though you've made a hash of this and a mash of that? Of course, you do. Do you deserve it even though you were to blame for that terrible A, even though you were the cause of that horrible B, and even though you didn't help when it came to that awful C? Of course, you do. By purchasing it and by sitting in it, you are announcing that you are human, and that, warts and all, you deserve some ease.

You aren't after ease for its own sake. By living more easily inside, relaxing better, pestering yourself less, by finally getting off that bed of nails, you position yourself for self-improvement. It is easier to be your best you when your mind isn't being jabbed continually!

Your easy chair is your place for relaxation, rejuvenation, daydreams, bursts of imagination, forgiveness, hard thinking, renewed hope, and everything else better done in an easy chair than on a bed of nails. No doubt you agree, and yet it may prove hard to part with your bed of nails. It exists in your mind because, for the longest time, you've been certain that you deserve it. Part of you is positive that you ought to punish yourself for all those messes, mistakes, and missteps.

Maybe you have some lingering feeling that you deserve that bed of nails. You don't. Maybe something about it feels downright comfortable. Break that spell. Sleeping on that bed of nails only makes matters worse, not better. If you want to expiate your guilt, then do a good deed, say a kind word, and make a difference.

It is past time to discard that bed of nails and replace it with an easy chair. Focus on this work and do not move on to another chapter until you've called the haulers! Get that bed of nails out of there!

By the way, it doesn't have to be an easy chair. Maybe that isn't exactly the right image for you. If easy chairs suggest old folks and decrepitude, pick a different image. Throughout this adventure of ours, please pick images that work for you. This is the redesign of *your* mindroom. Decorate it and design it as you like! Does a loveseat better suit you than an easy chair? Then a loveseat it is!

When you form an intention, like replacing that bed of nails with an easy chair, there are two excellent additional steps to take after visualizing the change. One is to begin to actively think thoughts that support that intention. Here, for example, are five thoughts that support that intention:

1. "No bed of nails for me!"
2. "I love my easy chair!"
3. "I am worthy."
4. "Lightness and ease."
5. "I am becoming more self-friendly."

Imagine entering your mindroom, throwing open the windows, enjoying the soft breeze, exclaiming, "I love my easy chair!" and sitting down in it to think, dream, imagine, or remember. Isn't that the ticket!

Second, you can support an intention by engaging in new behaviors. Here, for example, are five behaviors that support your intention to replace your usual self-pestering with a new self-friendly lightness and ease:

1. Notice which of your behaviors seem to come from a self-unfriendly place. To begin with, just notice.

2. Pick one behavior that looks to be coming from that self-unfriendly place. Give yourself the following instruction: "The next time I'm about to behave in that way, I'm going to visit my mindroom, get comfy in my easy chair, and see if that makes a difference."

3. When you feel yourself about to behave in that self-unfriendly way, visualize that bed of nails being hauled away. Wave goodbye to it. See if that makes a difference.

4. Repeat this process with another behavior that looks to be coming from that same self-unfriendly place.

5. Continue the process of identifying self-unfriendly behaviors and countering each with those two visualizations: the bed of nails being hauled away, and you comfy in your easy chair.

Nothing is more important to change than the ways that we diminish, derail, defeat, and inflict pain on ourselves. Turn your brilliance to this subject of self-inflicted pain. You might try asking the question "Why do I do that?" from a different perspective, say, from one of an evolutionary biologist or an evolutionary psychologist. Hazard some fascinating guesses about why human beings engage in all that self-unfriendly self-infliction. Don't worry if those aren't your fields of expertise—try some imaginative guessing. Your guess may be as good as the experts'!

· ✛ ○ ✛ ·

> **Visualization:** Visualize removing your bed of nails and replacing it with an easy chair.
>
> **Writing Prompt:** What odd bits of your original nature may you have to contend with as you try to redesign your mindroom?

PUTTING UP NEW WALLPAPER

Right behind your everyday thoughts and feelings—even when those thoughts and feelings are relatively lighthearted and self-friendly—there may reside a constant background coloration of sadness.

That's true for an awful lot of people. It's as if they'd painted the walls of their mindroom the most depressing shade of gray imaginable, or soot from a coal fire had continually deposited itself on those walls since they were little children. What can be done about all that background sadness?

Well, put up new wallpaper, of course!

First, let's get those walls prepped and get all that soot off! Fire up your power washer and clean those walls. Watch all that soot disappear down the drain. It's lucky that in your mindroom, you can power wash your walls without getting anything wet! There go a lifetime of regrets and disappointments. There go the failures, the harm done to you, the sludge of missed opportunities and broken promises. Isn't it quite something to see those walls clean again?

Now, pick out your new wallpaper. Pull out some gorgeous imaginary wallpaper books, sit in your easy chair, and peruse the patterns: floral ones, Victorian ones, graphical ones, ones that remind you of Mondrian, hypermodern ones, Gothic ones, super-simple ones, ornate ones resembling cake decorations. What shall it be? Which one cheers you up and warms your heart the most? That's the one!

Hanging real wallpaper is no easy feat. But hanging this wallpaper is a breeze! Watch it go up without a wrinkle or bubble in sight. While you're at it, throw open your windows and let a good breeze float in. If wallpaper doesn't do it for you, then paint your walls some colors you love. Create exactly the bright, cheerful walls you want. This is your room and you can paint it or wallpaper it any way you like!

There's more to do, too, in addition to putting up new wallpaper or painting your walls, if you want to get rid of a lifetime of sadness. Let's summarize a bit. You've installed windows so as to let in a breeze, some fresh air, and some fresh thoughts. Throwing open those windows will help with the sadness. We got rid of that bed of nails and replaced it with an easy chair—surely that easy chair will make for a happier mental environment. And we have many more things to try in the coming chapters that will help reduce that background sadness.

Each of these efforts will help you improve the landscape of your mind. The major shift I'm suggesting is the shift from the idea that you are merely a creature who thinks thoughts, to the truer idea that you can enter into a brilliant new relationship with your own brain. By employing the metaphor of a room, by visualizing that room and its contents, and by stocking it with what you need and deserve—bright walls, an easy chair, windows that open, and all the rest—you get yourself mentally healthy and keep yourself that way.

Most people live in a cell and are their own jailer. You can switch out that prison cell for a room as pleasant, beautiful, and functional as you would like to make it. I hope you like the wallpaper you chose! And if you don't, switch it right out!

Visualization: Visualize repainting or repapering the walls of your mindroom so that it is a more cheerful place to inhabit.

Writing Prompt: How will you keep track of the changes that you're making to your mindroom? Give that some thought and write on that theme.

INSTALLING A SAFETY VALVE

Let's step back for a moment.

You understand that we are not actually moving furniture or stripping walls. "Mindroom" is a metaphor. Because it is a metaphor, it provides us with maximum flexibility. One reader might want to consider all of the changes that I'm suggesting and make all of them. Another reader might focus on making one specific change or running with one particular idea. From my point of view, if you really engage with even just one of these visualizations—for instance, getting rid of that bed of nails and replacing it with an easy chair—you will have done yourself a world of good. This chapter's visualization is a case in point. If you get clear on the idea I'm about to discuss and you make use of that visualization, you will greatly reduce your stress levels.

Human beings find themselves pressured in all sorts of ways. And these pressures are experienced *as pressure*, as the sort of pressure that brings on migraines. To simply and brilliantly deal with these real and insistent pressures, install a release valve somewhere in your mindroom. You might visualize this as releasing the pressure from a pressure cooker, releasing steam from a boiler, or opening a vacuum-sealed can and enjoying that familiar *pop*. Take a moment and consider how you might want to visualize "releasing pressure." Try to get a clear picture in your mind's eye.

You might accompany what you see with the mantra: "Releasing pressure now." You might create a small ceremony where you let the pressure out through your mouth with a *whoosh!* When you begin to do that releasing regularly, you will find yourself doing a much better job of managing your mania, your unproductive obsessions, your addictive behaviors, and the other consequences that result from not releasing mind pressure soon enough or well enough.

Please try to make personal sense of this metaphor of a safety or pressure release valve. Think of how important it really is to accomplish this release. What is "obsessive-compulsive disorder" but the playing out of a certain sort of mind pressure? The same goes for addiction. Isn't the essence of addiction the *pressure* to drink alcohol, the *pressure* to gamble, the *pressure* to incessantly check our email? Isn't pressure the driving force behind all addictions? What if you had a safety or release valve that worked to instantly release that pressure? Wouldn't that be *something*?

The same applies to mania and other pressurized internal states like it. Isn't mania a pressurized fleeing from something, like meaninglessness, or a pressurized racing toward something, like hoped-for meaning? And what about anxiety? Think of the *pressure* you experience before an important performance. These pressures drive many, if not most, of the so-called "mental disorders" that plague people. What better help than a release valve to reduce that pressure by allowing it to harmlessly escape!

Maybe "pressure cooker" doesn't capture your experience of pressure. If it doesn't, then maybe "safety valve" or "pressure release valve" aren't the right metaphors for you to employ. What image better captures your experience of mental pressure? Maybe it's a malfunctioning diving suit or spacesuit? Then your visualization may be that diving suit or spacesuit being *instantly* repaired. You can breathe again! Just like that, the immense pressure of the deep ocean or empty space no longer troubles you. That's the beauty of visualization: you can see all of that at warp speed, both the rent in the fabric *and* the repair.

Maybe it's a jackhammer hammering that best captures your experience of internal pressure and noise. Then install a wall switch that, when flipped, immediately silences that jackhammer. Practice flipping that wall switch. Pounding. Silence. Pounding. Silence. Don't leave that visualization until you've gotten adept at silencing that jackhammer and creating blessed silence and peace.

Set the intention to reduce the pressure you're experiencing, then consciously and mindfully align your thoughts with that intention. Here are five thoughts that support your intention to reduce and release mind pressure:

1. "I know how to release this pressure."
2. "I don't have to rush to act just because I feel pressured to act."
3. "Time to use my safety valve!"
4. "Releasing pressure now!"
5. "Whoosh!"

Here are five behaviors that support your intention to release and reduce mind pressure:

1. Choose a small object to carry with you—a special coin, a polished stone—and when you feel that pressure building up in you, take out your coin or stone, rub it as you might rub a talisman, and say, "Releasing pressure now!"

2. Identify some of the stressors that create pressure in your life. See if any of them can be eliminated. For those that can't be eliminated, use your safety valve *in a daily way* to reduce the amount of pressure they produce.

3. Investigate which everyday activities, like hot showers or walks in nature, serve to reduce your experience of pressure. Make sure to include these activities in your daily routine.

4. See if some change—whether as large as changing careers, as medium-sized as avoiding a toxic family member, or as small as not watching violent television shows before bed—may help reduce your mind pressure.

5. Ask yourself the question, "What do I need to do in order to reduce this pressure?" If an answer comes to you, take your own advice!

There is no task more important than figuring out how to reduce the pressure that plagues us all. Use your brilliance to dream up your own idiosyncratic pressure-reduction strategies. If you're a mechanical engineer or a physicist, what might you take away from your knowledge of pressure in the physical world that might prove useful in handling your mental pressure? If you're a singer/songwriter, is there a ballad or anthem to write and sing? Use your brilliance to meet this challenge!

As a final visualization, picture yourself traveling deep into your being, through your arteries and your veins, on a journey to the source of this terrible pressure. Pass all the civilized thoughts and measured feelings and go deeper into that fantastic tangle, roaring through tunnels and dropping precipitously, until you reach…the source. What do you see there, face-to-face with the source of this terrible pressure? Now that you see it, can you just snap your fingers and make it vanish?

Visualization: Visit your mindroom. Decide where you will keep your safety valve and how you will use it.

Writing Prompt: Play with the word "pressure" and with the phrases "safety valve" and "pressure release valve." See what they conjure and what you learn.

ADDING A CALMNESS SWITCH

Let's get a new habit in place. When you enter the room that is your mind, flip on the switch by the door. This turns on the lights. This gesture can also accomplish a second thing: producing instant calmness. Let's have that light switch double as a calmness switch.

Our anxiety, our agitation, and our racing brain prevent us from living the life we would like to live. We can't visit our favorite faraway places if we're afraid to fly. We can't live our dream of performing if we're too anxious to perform. We can't make our best decisions if our brain is racing and our nerves are jangling. Achieving needed calmness by simply flipping a switch will help you achieve your other mental health goals as well.

Maybe you can't change your anxious nature or eliminate all the distress and agitation arising from your past traumas by engaging in a single mental exercise of this sort. But you will have to pick a starting point if you want to change your anxious nature and reduce that agitation, and this is a wonderful place to start. Turn on the lights whenever you enter your mindroom and feel calmer at the same time by virtue of having flipped that switch.

Have a conversation with yourself about this idea. Explain to yourself, "It's odd, but I think I get it. I can become genuinely calmer by just deciding to become calmer." When something happens to raise your anxiety level today—a problem at work, something you encounter in the news, a problem with your current creative project, some family matter, or one of your chronic pestering thoughts—take a deep breath and say, "I'm practicing calmness. Let me flip that calmness switch and deal with this calmly."

This is a simple, excellent way to manifest your love for yourself and to more powerfully stand behind your life-purpose choices. When we allow ourselves to be pulled around by the nose by our own frayed nerves, boiling blood, and racing brain, we can't be the person we intend to be. Calmness is a bedrock value that promotes all the other values we want to uphold.

Practice the following:

- When that hunger builds up in you to eat anything and everything and to throw your diet out the window, say, "I am practicing calmness. Let me flip that calmness switch and deal with this calmly."

- When your mate does that particular thing that always drives you crazy and is about to provoke a fight that you know will lead nowhere, say, "I am practicing calmness. Let me flip that calmness switch and deal with this calmly."

- When the novel you're writing stalls because you don't know what happens next, instead of bad-mouthing yourself or abandoning the project, say, "I am practicing calmness. Let me flip that calmness switch and deal with this calmly."

- When that craving to start drinking builds up in you, do all the things you know to do as part of your recovery program and also say, "I am practicing calmness. Let me flip that calmness switch and deal with this calmly."

- When you feel that terrible heaviness and emptiness because life has suddenly lost all meaning and you know that the deep sadness that dogs your heels is about to descend, rather than rushing off manically to do something to forestall that feeling or taking to your bed and pulling the covers up over your head, say, "I am practicing calmness. Let me flip that calmness switch and deal with this calmly."

Of course, in each of these cases there is more to do than just tell yourself to be calm. Calmness alone will not stop you from overeating, improve your relationship with your mate, allow you to finish your novel, ward off a drinking binge, or keep existential sadness completely at bay. However, it is a valuable first step and may even make all the difference.

You can increase the calmness in your life in many different ways. Thinking thoughts that calm you, rather than agitate you, is crucial. Removing stressors from your life will help, as will a useful relaxation technique or a simple breathing technique, but nothing is simpler than creating a calmness switch. Learn to flip it when needed in the direction of calmness. You can associate this idea with our metaphor of "the room that is your mind" by having the switch that flips on the lights in your mindroom double as a calmness switch. Give it a try!

· + ○ + ·

Visualization: Visualize installing a calmness switch and using it.

Writing Prompt: In addition to your calmness switch, what two or three other anxiety management strategies might you add to your repertoire of anxiety management skills?

HANGING A PAINTING OF APRICOTS

We're chatting about your mindroom as if it were a physical place. That's the metaphor we're employing. In that physical place, all sorts of processes play themselves out. There are the complicated processes of thinking, remembering, imagining, and so on. Everything that a mind can do, it does in that mindroom. These complicated, dynamic processes are in fact complicated and dynamic *processes*, and it turns out that human beings have a very hard time tolerating process. Let's look at just one process that is so very important to anyone who creates or does intellectual work: the creative process.

The creative process is much harder to tolerate than most people imagine (creatives included). It is hard to tolerate for all of the following reasons and for many more as well:

- Only a percentage of the work that we do turns out well, and only a percentage of that percentage is really excellent, meaning that we have many "failed" efforts to endure. That's the reality of process.

- The creative process involves making one choice after another (for instance, "Should I send my character here, or should I send my character there?"). Choosing provokes anxiety, and who likes anxiety?

- The creative process involves going into the unknown, which can prove scary, especially if where we are going is into the recesses of our own psyche. How much of that roiling can we endure?

- The tasks we set ourselves—unraveling this scientific knot, creating this full-scale opera—may be beyond our intellectual or technical capabilities or may require information and understanding that we don't currently possess. The reality is that we may not prove equal to realizing our goals.

- The thing called "inspiration"—one of the great joys of the creative process, without which our work would prove lifeless—comes only periodically and can't be produced on demand. The reality is that inspiration is intermittent, and when it isn't there, we have to do our work anyway.

One reason the creative process can feel so daunting is that not everything creatives attempt will turn out beautifully. Many efforts will turn out just ordinary, and a significant number will prove to be flat-out terrible. A composer writes a hit Broadway musical and their next one is abysmal. No one can believe it's the same person! A novelist pens a brilliant first novel and their second one is unreadable. What a disappointment! A physicist comes *this close* to a breakthrough, but they don't break through, rendering their several years of work "worthless." How demoralizing! These are everyday occurrences in the lives of creatives, and they're the rule rather than the exception. *This is the process.*

What to do? Of course, do everything required to make the work good, including getting quiet, showing up, honestly appraising, and all the rest. But in addition to all that, we must maturely accept the reality of missteps, mistakes, messes, unhappy outcomes, lost weeks, and even lost years.

To help with this effort at maturity, do the following: hang a still life painting of a bowl of apricots on a wall of your mindroom. Have that bowl be filled with gorgeous, ripe apricots and also with mottled, discolored, overripe apricots.

Have some of those apricots be downright rotten. The lesson of this painting? *That you must calmly and gracefully take the bad with the good.*

A romantic painter would surely paint only gorgeous apricots. Likewise, a super-realist painter in preparing their still life for copying would include just the best apricots, unless they were intending to make a point about decay. Virtually no painter, past or present, would fill their bowl with beautiful *and* rotten apricots. That goes against our ingrained ideas about beauty and about what a painting is "supposed to do."

The painting you hang, however, is not being hung for its beauty. It is being hung there to remind you about the reality of the process. It is being hung there to remind you that you must take the bad with the good as you create. It is being hung there to remind you to be your most mature self, the you who understands that you are bound to produce work all along the spectrum, from lousy to brilliant.

Among his hundreds of cantatas, Bach's most famous cantata is number 140. His top ten would likely be numbers 4, 12, 51, 67, 80, 82, 131, 140, 143 and 170. What about the others? Are some merely workmanlike and unmemorable? Yes. Are some not very interesting at all? Yes? Was Bach obliged to live with that reality? Yes—as must you. You might produce a brilliant first thing and then never try again, ensuring your success rate remains at 100 percent. But is that a way to live a life? Rather, is that a way to avoid living?

Hang a painting of a bowl of apricots filled with lovely ripe apricots and unlovely blemished, overripe apricots in a prominent place on one of the walls of your mindroom. The painting is not there to reprimand you, chastise you, or discourage you. Rather, it is there to remind you about the reality of the process, a reality that no human being can escape or evade.

Every once in a while, maybe when your creative or intellectual work is going poorly, or when you've created something that fails to meet your standards, stand in front of that painting, sigh, and murmur, "Process." Process is what it is. Honoring its reality and calmly living with it are choices you get to make.

· ✢ ○ ✢ ·

Visualization: Visualize a painting of a bowl filled with both gorgeous apricots and rotten apricots.

Writing Prompt: Think deeply about the word "process." Describe how "process" really works in some aspect of your life, as opposed to how you wish it would work.

CREATING A NO-STUMBLE ZONE

Human beings repeatedly stumble in exactly the same spots. They marry an abusive mate, divorce them, and marry another one. They fail to prepare for an important audition, they don't win the audition, and fail to prepare for the next one. They dread going to the dentist and drink heavily to deal with their anxiety; when the next appointment looms, they drink heavily again. It is one of our most human traits to repeatedly stumble in exactly the same spots, over and over again.

What's to be done? Create a no-stumble zone in your mindroom! Off in a corner, maybe cordoned off, create a perfectly flat, pristine, object-free surface where stumbling is just about impossible.

Imagine that you are doing a beautiful job of maintaining your mental health and emotional well-being, and up comes a trip to the dentist, a visit from your mother, a broken promise by your mate, or some extra work at your job. Here it comes— that place where you regularly trip and fall.

You know that the visit to the dentist will not only trigger panic, but it will completely change your personality—from the person you've been working on becoming to that other person who lived out of control for the whole decades of their twenties and thirties.

You know that the impending visit from your mother will create an extraordinary amount of lethargy and sadness in your system, make you hyper-critical, and leave you with a bad taste for weeks after she's left.

You know that another promise broken by your mate will create all sorts of bad feelings in you and between the two of you, including revenge fantasies, doubts about the viability of the relationship, thoughts about leaving, and a bout of severe sadness.

You know that your job is already only barely tolerable. When your boss springs extra work on you on some Friday afternoon, forcing you to have to catch the last train home, that will ruin your weekend, cause you to yell at your mate and your children, and almost cause you to kick the dog.

In recovery work, this "impending event" is called a trigger. A trigger for someone who trips and falls around alcohol might be the annual holiday party at work, a visit from an old drinking buddy, or a business situation that puts them among heavy drinkers. In recovery programs, you're taught to identify these triggers, take them seriously, and know clearly what you will do when you are triggered or about to be triggered.

If you know from past experience that this impending event will trip you up, that means you have good warning and can try something to prevent that trip and fall. That "something" could be anything you know to do that keeps you from tripping repeatedly over the very same crack in the pavement. The simplest thing may be to visit your mindroom's cordoned-off no-tripping zone, halt in front of the big warning sign alerting you to watch your step, and as a result, not trip.

For someone in recovery, that "something to do" may be calling your sponsor or attending a twelve-step meeting. Maybe you skip the holiday party or see your old buddy only in the safety of your own home or let your coworkers know that you are in recovery and can't hang out with them. Maybe you would do several of these things, or maybe you would do all of these things—including using the no-stumble zone you've created.

Picture one of your triggers—that visit to the dentist, that visit from your mother. Examine it without flinching. Adamantly say, "I'm not tripping there," and explain to yourself what you will do to handle that specific challenge when it looms on the horizon. We journey through life on a road defined by its unevenness. It is buckled in places and is bound to buckle more, creating countless chances for us to trip and fall. We will come to know some of these cracks only by tripping over them; but many of them are visible from a distance, and we can prepare ourselves so as to not trip and fall.

Wouldn't that prove a welcome relief and spare you any number of bruises? Not tripping and falling repeatedly over the same challenges and obstacles is a lovely habit to learn. As much work as we may do on ourselves to keep us mentally healthy, we can still be triggered and lose our balance. When you see one of these triggers coming, take it seriously. Off you go to your no-stumble zone, where (in no danger of tripping) you get to marshal your resources and create your tactical plan.

· + ○ + ·

Visualization: Visualize a no-stumble zone where you can go to safely consider how to avoid repetitive stumbles.

Writing Prompt: Why do you think that human beings have so much trouble learning from experience? Why do they repeatedly trip over that same crack in the sidewalk?

SECTIONING OFF A COMPARISON-FREE ZONE

When we compare ourselves to others, we create emotional pain. For creatives and performing artists, the folks with whom I've been working for the past thirty-five years, nothing eats at them more than envy. Someone they went to school with gets a big award and they can hardly function for the next six months. This is a so-very-human weakness, to be deeply affected and even disabled by envy.

Say that you're a visual artist. You're likely to occasionally find yourself in one of the following situations:

- You enter a juried competition. One of your paintings is accepted and, although you discover that you didn't win a coveted ribbon, you nevertheless attend the gala opening of the exhibition.
- You attend a large trade show where artist materials of every conceivable sort are displayed, and where well-known artists give technique and material demonstrations, some of which you attend.
- You spend a week at the annual or biennial convention of your medium, like the biennial International Association of Pastel Societies (IAPS) Convention. There, you take workshops and get to see the juried and award-winning work of well-known artists.

What are some of the psychological repercussions of attending events of this sort? Typically, there are both powerful positive emotions and powerful negative emotions generated by such attendance. Not so long ago I spent four days in Albuquerque at the IAPS Convention, where I gave the keynote address. I talked with many artists, and here's what I heard.

These artists were inspired to be among other pastel artists who had come from all over the world—China, Europe, Australia, New Zealand, Canada, etc.—and who constituted their tribe. Often isolated in their individual studios, they loved the camaraderie, the shared love of the medium of pastel, the excitement of learning about new products, and the sheer fun of the lively events organized throughout the convention.

At the same time, they couldn't keep themselves from doing a lot of comparing. The juried exhibition that was a featured part of the convention contained one beautiful work after another. It was hard for the less experienced artists—even for many of the pros—to stop themselves from saying, "Wow, that's better than what I do." Many artists told me that they were leaving the convention with very mixed emotions: they felt inspired on the one hand, and quite demoralized on the other.

It would be lovely if we never fell victim to envy and never compared ourselves to others. But that is probably beyond us. Do the next best thing and create a comparison-free zone in your mindroom. It might even be a whole second room with its own furnishings and fixtures. In this room, no comparisons are permitted. When you sit on the sofa in this room, you never hear yourself saying, "Bob is doing so well," or "Mary has such great technique." You only hear yourself saying things like "What does my work need from me today?" and "I can't wait to get to my work!"

Among my clients who have the hardest time with this are those that keep track of their peers' successes. They know who's won which prize, whose new book has just been published to rave reviews, whose music video has crossed a hundred million views, and whose solo show sold out. Often, they will claim to simply be keeping up with industry news, as if news of that sort had no negative psychological repercussions. It is almost as if they were testing themselves: *let me see if I can tolerate hearing about the success of others without falling apart.* They are about as successful at that as is an alcoholic who tests themselves by spending every night in a bar.

One client, a singer/songwriter, fixated on the touring schedule of a relatively well-known independent recording artist who regularly traveled worldwide. My client knew this artist's schedule virtually by heart—a London venue, followed by a Brighton venue, followed by a Manchester venue, followed by stops in Wales and Scotland, then off to Paris. While paying all this attention to the other artist, they paid no attention to landing gigs of their own. Was it easier and safer to be envious of their putative rival than to put themselves out into the world?

Indeed, almost nothing is harder than letting go of fixations of this sort. Keep comparisons to a minimum. To that end, create a dedicated space your mindroom where no comparisons are permitted and visit it the *instant* you feel a comparison approaching. It would be a shame if you had to stop attending industry events or missed out on visiting with your tribe just because the negative emotions that such events generated became too hard to handle. Likewise, it would be a shame if you used such comparing to sabotage yourself and keep yourself from succeeding. Instead, when you find yourself succumbing to or indulging in comparisons, hurry to that comparison-free zone in your mindroom and declare an immediate end to it.

· + ○ + ·

Visualization: Visualize a comparison-free zone where no comparisons are permitted.

Writing Prompt: If you have trouble preventing yourself from comparing yourself to others, what, in addition to creating a comparison-free zone in your mindroom, might you try to get over that habit?

HANGING UP YOUR STRAITJACKET

I see personality as being made up of three constituents: original personality, formed personality, and available personality. I'll chat more about this model in a future chapter. Here, I'd like you to get the following image in mind: a formed personality operates like a straitjacket. We stiffen over time into our repetitive, "regular" selves; unless and until we make some changes, we are obliged to operate from that stiff place, without much room to move or breathe.

Likewise, the modern world straightjackets us. If you're smart, sensitive, and creative, you're likely to want to manifest all that potential in you. But the modern world is designed to restrict your options and straitjacket your efforts. There is no contemporary category of "general thinker" that matches the ancient job title of "natural philosopher," where one could do science, philosophy, art, and anything else that caught one's fancy. Nowadays you must do something much smaller than that.

A smart person today must become a clear something—a college professor specializing in the early works of Melville, an engineer specializing in bridges, a lawyer who knows the ins and outs of tax law, and so on. Having become that something, they must stay right there, trapped needing to prepare another journal article, pondering another bend in the river, or familiarizing themselves with another tax code change. How existentially debilitating is that?

Marilyn, a client and a biological researcher, explained to me:

"The journey to get where I am today as a biological researcher at a prestigious university was long and hard. Because it was so hard, with so many hurdles to jump over and hoops to jump through, I never noticed exactly what was happening. I never noticed that in some of my undergraduate classes, I was actually excited by the material and actually enjoyed thinking about the big questions. But as each year progressed and as I had to narrow my focus, find my niche, and choose my life form, as it were (I've ended up an expert on a certain worm), I stopped thinking and spent my days in pretty dreary fashion trying to find some enthusiasm for my own research. Biology is amazing, and yet it has all come together in a very disappointing way."

Martin, a client and a philosophy professor, described his situation in the following way:

"I've spent the last two months defending a journal article I wrote about praise and blame in Kantian ethics from the three peer reviewers who nitpicked it to death. In order to have a chance at getting it published, I need to address every one of their trivial concerns. And the problem for me isn't so much that I'm spending all of my time on what feels like a silly and mind-numbing task, but rather that this is the box I've put myself in. This exact box, where I make some fine logical or linguistic distinctions and then have to act like that matters, like I am increasing human knowledge or something.

"The academy is a comfortable place to be and I suppose that I could turn myself into someone who does think bigger than I currently think. But I don't. I don't know what the problem is: if it's the system, philosophy itself that I don't believe in, a lack of genuine interest in thinking, a lack of confidence, a fear of biting off more than I can chew, or what. All I know is this: can I really do this for twenty or thirty more years? That seems completely unbearable."

What can you possibly do if this is the sort of challenge you're facing, that your formed personality and life-as-you-are-living-it both straitjacket you? A step in the direction of a possible solution is the following. Physically remove that straitjacket that is forcing you to work small, think small, and be small. Like a Houdini, slip right out of it. Go to the room that is your mind, create a closet or a storage chest, wriggle out of your straitjacket, and hang it up or store it away.

Feel freer!

You may have to put that straitjacket back on when you go back to the lab tomorrow, but for this evening you can wander anywhere in biology you like. You may have to put it back on tomorrow when you're obliged to defend your article on Kantian ethics, but for this evening you can think as broadly as Plato, Aristotle, or one of the pre-Socratic philosophers you admire so much. At the very least, you'll be able to spend a few blissful, unbound hours. Enjoy and revel in them!

The challenges that smart, sensitive, creative people face when it comes to finding meaningful employment, surviving dull, routine work, avoiding a lifetime in a claustrophobic corner of a given profession, choosing between work that pays and work that interests them, and generally adapting their smarts to the contours of society's configurations are never-ending. You may prove to be one of the lucky ones, make an excellent match, and never feel straightjacketed. As likely as not, however, you will find yourself among the majority of folks who perennially find that the world is designed to restrict their thinking and restrain their talents. If you are among this multitude, at least you can remove that straitjacket for some hours at a time, and for those hours, you can breathe and think more freely.

· ✦ ○ ✦ ·

Visualization: Visualize removing the straitjacket of formed personality and the straitjacket of life-as-you-are-living-it and experience a period of freedom.

Writing Prompt: Describe in your own words the difference between the two straightjackets I described: the straitjacket of your formed personality and the straitjacket of your life-as-you-are-living-it.

INCLUDING A GRANDEUR CORNER

We tend to associate the word "grandeur" with events like royal weddings and sights like the Grand Canyon. Hotels are grand, canyons are grand, and cruise ships are grand, but something about that way of thinking prevents us from demanding grandeur from the other stuff of existence, like an image that we craft, a jam that we jar, or a kiss that we give. For more reasons than we can count, the traditional concept of grandeur isn't very present in our daily lives.

In all the meetings I've ever attended—faculty meetings, business meetings, meetings of therapists, and meetings of artists—I've never heard anyone say, "What's wanted is a little more grandeur." Have you? On the long list of things discussed when people gather, grandeur never appears. There are no parties honoring it, no organizations devoted to it, no lobbyists buttonholing members of Congress and whispering, "Support the grandeur bill and we'll make it worth your while!"

I remember sitting in a sterile break room in a suite of offices, writing by hand before the class I taught began. In a corner of the room were some boxes of computer parts. There was a soda machine, a microwave, a copy machine, a fire extinguisher, a sink, a wastepaper basket, and a metal cabinet for office supplies. The walls were a dull blue-gray, as were the round table at which I sat, the chairs, and the floor. But on the wall across from me was a poster of a Manuel Neri oil-on-paper called *Alberica No. 1*. It portrayed a woman with a blue face, a yellow torso, and burgundy legs. The top half of the background was a brilliant yellow and the bottom half was a striking blue. If I hadn't had it or something like it on the wall to look at, I would surely have died of grandeur deprivation in a room like that.

Think about your own life. What last stirred feelings of grandeur in you? Was it something you saw on the commute to your day job, some reality show episode, or something you experienced at a meeting? Probably not. My hunch is that you were last stirred by music, a film, a passage in a book, or a piece of art. You stopped, listened to the music, and said to yourself, "How beautiful!" or "How powerful!" or "This is good stuff!" You were transported. In the back of your mind, you whispered, "I should be creating and doing work this strong." You said to yourself, but maybe not in such a way that you could hear the message clearly, "Without this beauty I would die."

The painter Max Beckmann once said:

> "All important things in art have always originated from the deepest feeling about the mystery of Being."

I think that this sentiment comes close to capturing the origins of our sense of grandeur. We are built to appreciate mystery, to harbor deep feelings, to contemplate the universe with its marvelous quirks and distinguishing features. To bring less than all of this to life is to bring only a shadow of our inheritance. Without Neri on the wall, Mozart in the air, or Tolstoy in our hands, we would wither away, no matter how good the benefits and stock options are at our day job. We need grandeur to survive.

You can remind yourself of this necessity by installing a grandeur corner in your mindroom. Here, you freely and deeply hold the intention to create something powerful, beautiful, admirable, meaningful, resonant, and grand. You remind yourself that grandeur is available and that you can create it yourself. What is actually in such a corner? That's for you to decide. Maybe it's filled with music. Maybe on a chalkboard is the scientific formula that always stirs you. Maybe you'll choose items that evoke feelings of awe, grandeur, and mystery. What do you think?

Create your grandeur corner now. Visit the room that is your mind, look around, pick a suitable nook or corner, and fill it in such a way that what you experience as you face it is grandeur. Nothing in your grandeur corner may look grand in any traditional sense. I'd be surprised if you installed marble staircases and velvet drapes. You might even find very homey objects there: a stone from a river bed, a whimsical doll, a door somehow made grand by its layers of peeling paint.

By redesigning your mind, you give yourself the opportunity to honor aspects of existence that usually get overlooked as you rush through life. Grandeur is one of those aspects. On an ordinary day, life can be drab, unexciting, and uninviting. There may nothing at all "out there" that promotes a feeling like grandeur. That being the case, you will have to promote such feelings from within. Create your grandeur corner and pencil experiencing it onto your calendar.

· + O + ·

Visualization: Visualize a grandeur corner—a dedicated place in your mindroom where you can go to experience some awe, mystery, magic, and grandeur.

Writing Prompt: What feelings like grandeur would you like to experience more often? Think about how you might redesign your mindroom so as to support and provoke those feelings.

WEARING YOUR MATTERING SWEATER

It would seem self-evident that a person would decide to matter and consider their efforts, if not dramatically important, at least not pointless. Why wouldn't a person opt to matter and conceptualize their efforts as valuable?

Well, certainly, their upbringing might be one impediment. They might have grown up lectured about the extent to which they didn't matter and punished for attempting to matter. Their culture, too, may have drilled into them the idea that they were merely one of many, and that group norms should always come first, religion should come first, fitting in should come first, and not making waves should come first. Many life lessons may have been taught to them about how wrong-headed, immoral, or pointless it is to opt to matter.

Still, the magnitude of their difficulty in opting to matter is not really explained, even by these many negative life lessons. It turns out that the main obstacle they face is the belief (shared by every modern person) that human life is "ultimately" meaningless. Any reasons that they try to adduce for mattering are overwhelmed by the possibility, bordering on a certainty, that they and their fellow human beings are only excited matter put on earth for no reason other than the universe could do it. All life (theirs included) is mere pointless happenstance, not worth crying about or taking seriously.

This bitter pill is a new view, barely two hundred years old. Before that, life seemed special. For thousands of years, the idea of life as categorically different from non-life, unique and important in the cosmos, was a core tenet of philosophy. This view felt compelling until biologists found that organic compounds could be created from inorganic materials, beginning with Wohler and the synthesis of urea in 1828.

We can date our present difficulties in making and maintaining meaning from that single event: the synthesis of urea. From that day forward, life lost much of its mystery, sanctity, importance, and glamour, and a new philosophy was needed. Once you join the scientific materialists (as all of us have done to a lesser or greater degree) and believe that you can make human beings simply by striking dead atoms with powerful but meaningless forces, life turns meaningless. This is the basic problem with which we've been wrestling for two hundred years. The suspicion that we do not matter haunts and plagues those of us who are existential, including believers.

We manage to bear up, despite the suspicion that we are merely excited matter. We find ways to bear up every day. But on many days, we discover that we can't bear up; on those days, we despair about our cosmic unimportance and grow furious with the facts of existence. We feel saddened and defeated, and we lose our motivation to make meaning in any way. The very word "meaning" strikes our ears as a cosmic joke. Because of our fear and the consequential grudge that we hold against the universe, we feel lost and alienated, like a refugee far from home in a universe that cares nothing for us.

What can help? Make the decision to matter and affirm that decision by, whenever you enter your mindroom, putting on your "I matter" sweater.

Visualize putting on a comfy sweater bearing the motto "I matter," or "My efforts matter," or some other phrase that communicates the idea that you must opt to matter, despite all your doubts about the universe. You put this imagined sweater on each time you enter your mindroom, perhaps right after flipping on the lights, flipping on your calmness switch, and using your safety valve to release a little pressure. Inside that room, you live in that sweater. With that sweater on, you remember to matter.

Every modern person is driven to throw up their hands and cry, "Why bother! Why try to wrestle this stupid novel into existence? I might as well eat chocolate and take a bubble bath. To hell with the ideas of life-purpose choosing and meaning-making!" So they eat chocolate and take a bubble bath. But within minutes, they are forcibly struck by the counter-thought that they are obliged to make meaning, and it feels so devoid of meaning to have thrown up their hands. A countervailing energy arises in them, something like hope or pride, an energy that readies them to combat their sincere belief that they are utterly unimportant. Wearing their mattering sweater is one way to defeat meaninglessness.

We must opt for life. We must opt to live the twenty years or the sixty years ahead of us. This may be all that we have, but it is exactly what we have. We force life to mean while we are alive and until death releases us from our responsibility to live authentically. We say, "While I am alive, I can love." We say, "While I am alive, I can learn a few things." We say, "While I am alive, I can help in some ways." We say, "While I am alive, I can create." We opt to matter because we can, and because, unromantically but utterly sincerely, we must.

Put on your mattering sweater. Rarely take it off.

Visualization: Visualize putting on your mattering sweater and wearing it as you go about your mindroom business.

Writing Prompt: For thousands of years, we've been burdened by the idea that we should "seek meaning." Instead, we should make meaning. Play with these ideas in writing.

PUTTING IN AN EXIT DOOR

We are often obliged to stay in our mindroom for protracted periods of time, maybe because we're trying to solve a personal problem, or maybe because we're creating something that demands intense, prolonged attention. That is all as it should be. But we must be careful not to overstay our welcome there.

Many people spend too much time in their mindroom worrying, obsessing, fretting, or just sitting there and thinking about nothing in particular. That isn't healthy or useful. What's needed? An exit door and an exit strategy! Your mind better have a clearly marked exit door, and you better know how and when to use it.

Let's put that in right now. Go to your mindroom, find the right spot, add an exit door, and clearly mark it! You want the sign over your exit door to brightly glow in the dark, just as the exit signs on airplanes do.

If you've ever found yourself buttonholed by someone who can't stop speaking, whose pressurized speech races on and on and who won't broach any interruption, you know that nothing at all can interfere with that person's agenda—whether that's convincing you that Martians abducted them, vaccinations ought to be made illegal, or that our youth today are self-indulgent and worthless. It won't help to exclaim, "Stop, enough!" It won't help to present some counterargument. It won't help to roll your eyes or make some "please stop!" gesture with your upraised palm. Your interlocutor is on a mission that has nothing to do with you, a mission to spill out the words that their mind is driving along with a whip.

Were you to exclaim "Stop!" they might actually stop for a split second, give you look of amazed incredulity—as if to say, "What, you don't think Martians are everywhere?"—and return immediately to their theme. Shake your head if you like, that won't phase them. To free yourself of their manic monologue, you must *leave*. There is absolutely nothing else to do. You must say, "Oh, I see Mary across the room and I haven't chatted with Mary in the longest time! It was so nice chatting with you." Then you bolt. Or maybe you skip any politeness—turn your back and just flee.

Your own mind can fail you in exactly that way. It can get on some bandwagon, usually under the pressure of some unacknowledged threat (for instance, that life feels meaningless and you don't want to notice that terrible shortfall), and jibber on about some theme that suddenly seems important beyond belief.

Maybe it's about how the walls are not quite the right shade of white and must be repainted this instant ("Navajo white, they should be Navajo white!"), or how it's imperative that you set off for South America on that vision quest that you've delayed thirty years, or how you really must tell your boss off in no uncertain terms this very morning. There your mind goes!

Such monologues are very hard to interrupt. There appears to be no "you" available at such tense times to say, "Bob, it's not about the walls," or "Calm down, this is not the year to run off to South America," or "Hold on, better to ask for a raise than to spit in his face."

What can you do when your mind is going on like that? Leave the monologue. That's the thing to do! Use the exit door you've installed and leave. Say to the "you" trapped listening to yourself go on and on, "I'm leaving now." Get up, turn your back on that manic monologue, get a firm grip on the doorknob, get your exit door opened, and stride into some sunny, blissful silence.

Once outside, as you walk in silence through a quiet garden in the direction of a café for some tea and a biscotti, you might dare to ask yourself, "What was that all about?" You were that manic speaker. Your mind produced that feverish monologue. No doubt, there is something to learn about why you felt compelled to go on that way. In the blissful silence of that garden walk, dare to quietly ask that poignant question: "What *was* that all about?"

These pressurized monologues arise all the time. Maybe you call them your obsessional thinking or your manic times, or maybe you don't have a name for them. Maybe they are just a part of you that you suppose you can't do much about. But there is something you can do. If you'd like to gain some freedom from pressure-driven monologues, you can create an exit door—maybe with a nice bit of red neon above the door that reads "Exit"—and leave whenever it would be wise for you to get out of there.

There are many other ways to handle manic energy, obsessional thinking, and the crises that bring them on. But isn't just leaving a refreshingly simple one? You quietly get up and leave—no need to remonstrate the speaker or announce your intentions. Then, there you suddenly are, in the silence of a lovely garden, on your way to an afternoon treat. Make sure that the room that is your mind is equipped with that exit door!

· + ○ + ·

Visualization: Install an exit door in your mindroom.

Writing Prompt: If you're caught up in some internal monologue and obsessively fretting about something, how will you get yourself moving toward the exit door you've installed? What tactic, strategy, mantra, or ceremony might you dream up to actually use your exit door when leaving your mindroom is the thing to do?

UNEMPLOYED JOHN

When working with a therapy client or a coaching client, I would never suggest that he or she stop everything so as to try out the forty plus visualizations I'm describing in this book. Rather, what happens is that, as we work together to unravel an issue, I may suggest one particular visualization that feels appropriate and helpful. Here and in the next chapter are two examples of how "redesigning your mind" gets translated into specifics as the work of therapy or coaching proceeds.

· ✦ ⭕ ✦ ·

When I was a psychotherapist, I worked with a client named John who came to see me because being unemployed was taking a heavy toll on him. He'd been unemployed for six months when I began seeing him, and his prospects were anything but rosy.

"I'm depressed," he said. "I've never been out of work for this long."

"Yes, this is making you sad. Were you also sad while you were at your job?"

"Yes! The job was depressing! I hated my boss, the hours were terrible, there were no chances for advancement, and I was just in a rut there, dreading to go to work."

I nodded. "How long were you at that job?"

"Six years."

"And the job before that one? How was that one?"

"Even worse! The whole environment was toxic. I had to get out of there!"

"How long were you at that job?"

"Eight years."

"And before that?"

"College."

"How was that?" I wondered.

"I had a hard time there. I didn't fit in very well, my roommate was uncommunicative, and I really didn't have any idea what I was doing there."

"Let me summarize," I said. "You are sad now. You were sad at your job. You were sad at the job before that. And you were sad in college. So you've been sad for, what, the last twenty years or so?"

John thought about that. "Yes, that sounds right. I've been clinically depressed that whole time?"

"Well, you've been sad that whole time," I replied with a smile. "And what about high school?"

"Oh my God! Let's not even talk about high school!"

"I wonder," I continued, "if we went all the way back if we wouldn't find the same thing: stomachaches, elementary school teachers you didn't like, feeling outside of things, and sadness. Is that what we'd find?"

"Yes," John agreed.

"So yes, you're unemployed. But the sadness isn't really just of this moment, is it? It's been a lifelong thing—maybe even a birth thing?"

"A birth thing?" This was clearly an idea he'd never encountered or considered before.

"Maybe you were born with certain sensitivities that opened you up to sadness right from the beginning. Who knows? But I don't want us to act like your 'depression' is just of this moment. Sadness has been with you for a very long time, hasn't it?"

"Yes, it has."

As we worked together, we focused on that lifelong sadness while addressing the practical matter of finding employment. It would have made no particular sense to suppose that John had contracted "the mental disorder of depression" as if he'd caught the flu. Nor would it have made any sense to suppose that something had "suddenly broken" somewhere inside of John. This sadness had been with him forever. Yes, unemployment was a present, pressing stressor in his life. But what was going on in John had been going on for a very long time and likely since birth. To fail to take that long view would be to fail to really see or know John.

I wondered if he might be willing to try a visualization at home between sessions. I described the basic idea of redesigning his mind so that it suited him better and felt better to inhabit, and I wondered if he might try two things: installing windows to let a breeze in, and repainting or repapering the walls of his mindroom.

At the next session, he was eager to share some news.

"I think I went overboard," he said. "I went to an actual wallpaper outlet. I almost couldn't find it, since it was buried in some industrial park. I spent the better part of half-a-day there! I didn't know what I was doing but I was in a good mood the whole time." He paused. "I didn't pick out any wallpaper. I don't think I was there to pick out any wallpaper. I think it was just my way of experiencing a little joy. Maybe, as you say, I was born sad. If so, then it's my job to find ways of feeling sunny. I don't think I'll be going back to that wallpaper outlet, but some ideas are percolating!"

· + ○ + ·

Visualization: I've presented you with a dozen redesign exercises so far. Take a glance back and see if one of them particularly speaks to you. If it does, spend time with it. Work on redesigning your mind in that one specific way. Enjoy yourself!

Writing Prompt: How might stressful and painful situations (like unemployment, divorce, political upheaval, etc.) increase the sadness that is already there, as opposed to being the "cause" of that sadness? Grapple a bit with that distinction.

ANGRY PATRICIA

Like most artists forced to work a day job, Paul Gauguin hated it. He ran off to Tahiti to paint and offered up the following mocking advice in his journal:

> "Why work? The gods are there to lavish upon the faithful the good gifts of nature."

An artist clear on how little chance they have to run off to Tahiti would happily throw a coconut at Paul's head if he wasn't already dead and buried. Still, when toiling away at their day job, an artist can't help but wonder, "Is this really the way I should be living?" Such was the question that a former client of mine, a painter named Patricia, couldn't get off her mind, saddled as she was with a forty-hour-a-week day job.

That day job—working in a Manhattan restaurant—hadn't seemed so terrible when she was in her twenties. Now that she'd turned thirty, it had become unbearable. She knew that she was lucky: the restaurant hadn't closed, as so many others had; meals there were expensive, which meant that her tips were large; and her immediate boss was no angel but no monster either. She knew that, as day jobs went, hers was pretty excellent. But it was still unbearable—and how little painting she was getting done!

To begin with, we could not come up with any great answers. Could she perhaps take a year off and live off parental money and do a lot of painting? No—her parents hated her decision to be an artist and absolutely would not support her, nor could she see herself asking them for money. Might another day job suit her better? No—this one was great, as day jobs went. Maybe she should train in some career and become a therapist, a life coach, or some other professional? No—how long that would take and how far that would take her from painting! Maybe, like in a romantic fantasy movie, she could snatch a rich man who would support her? How likely was that? Not very, nor was she very likely to stand for it! What then? Waste money on lottery tickets? Drink a lot and drown her sorrows?

We finally agreed on a short-term, six-month plan that focused on her getting more painting done—much more—and taking the demands of being a professional artist much more seriously. Did creating this plan allow her to give up her day job? No, of course not. It did, however, provide her with a glimmer of hope.

As might have been expected, the first month of the plan proved rocky. We agreed that she would check in via email every day, and she missed many days. Often on the days when she did check in, her messages amounted to "Didn't paint today." But the second month was better, and by the third month she was painting quite a bit, three and sometimes four times a week. Then she stopped abruptly.

"It's rage," she said at our next session.

Her situation enraged her. It enraged her that she had to work that day job. It enraged her that customers spent a hundred and fifty dollars a person for a meal at the restaurant where she worked. It enraged her that she had so many finished paintings accumulated but nothing to do with them. The commodification of art enraged her. What she saw in galleries enraged her. The world enraged her—more so every day.

But her rage ran even deeper and wider than all that. She hated the way her parents wrote her off and dismissed her desire to be a painter as indulgent and ridiculous—even though her father was a well-known painter! She hated how she had been bullied in childhood and made to feel scared by her father's rages and tantrums. She had a burning hatred for the world's cavalier injustices, the millions upon millions of shameless outrages perpetrated daily.

"How would you describe your relationship to that rage?" I wondered. "Are you 'for it' or 'against it'?"

She thought about. Then, after a long while, she said, "I'm attached to it."

That was a big-deal insight.

"And? Do you want to stay attached to it?"

"I'm not sure."

"Okay. Let's try the following."

I explained the idea of visualizing her mindroom and described a couple of changes that she might want to make to help release her anger. One visualization—hanging a still life painting of ripe and rotten apricots—captured her imagination. I could see her picturing it and thinking about it.

"Should I be angry that an apricot turns rotten?" she said after a while. She shook her head. "Maybe I can let go of some of this rage by focusing on process. You know...maybe I'll make some 'defaced apricot' paintings. I want to play with that idea. There's something there for me to learn."

She gave it a try, and it helped. She began quite enjoying painting her "defaced apricots," and she could feel herself detaching from at least a portion of her anger. The daily grind remained the daily grind for Patricia, but she continued painting. Then a gallery accepted two of her "defaced apricot" paintings. Shortly thereafter, one of them sold for its asking price. That wasn't the end of the story, of course; but it was a lovely landmark.

· ✛ ○ ✛ ·

Visualization: Create a visualization of your own. Imagine entering your mindroom and...

Writing Prompt: Can you change your environment in some way that would make it easier for you to enter and inhabit your mindroom?

DYNAMIC SELF-REGULATION

As we end Part I, let's pause and look at the super-interesting and super-important idea of dynamic self-regulation.

A brain's true brilliance is its ability to chat with itself, enter into self-conversation, and as a result of these conversations, engage in dynamic, system-wide self-regulation. Is anything in the universe more amazing than that? No brain feature is more important to you personally, since this dynamic self-regulation is the feature that allows for mental health and emotional well-being.

There are countless ways of think about human nature and what really makes us tick. Here are five typical approaches:

1. We are our biology. We are biological machines controlled by our genes, hormones, nervous system, and other aspects of biology. When, for example, we sustain a brain injury and lose our memory, that is one form of proof or evidence that we are our biology. The "medical model" view is that we are mentally healthy when our biology is functioning, and we are mentally unwell when our biology fails to function properly. In this view, we should treat mental distress as a biological matter requiring medical treatment, primarily medication.

2. As primarily psychological creatures, we are more or less held hostage by our brain. We act and experience as our mind develops, makes sense of our experiences and our circumstances, and manages our desires and

our instincts. In this view, we are mentally healthy when our mind refrains from distorting reality, stops creating unnecessary inner conflicts, refuses to succumb to emotional cravings, and so on—when, that is, it serves us rather than weakens us, harms us, or tyrannizes us. This view underpins psychotherapy, which is the second dominant mental health paradigm after the medical model paradigm.

3. We are this thing called personality. We are from birth, or we become over time, a formed creature who reacts repetitively and without thinking in ways determined by our genetic predispositions, the lessons we learn from our lived experiences, and our many diverse self-identity pieces. Each person is identifiable as fundamentally themselves. In common parlance, we describe people as introverts or extroverts, bubbly or melancholy, rigid or reckless, conventional or iconoclastic, or, in mental disorder language, passive-aggressive, borderline, and so forth. What's implied by these designations is the idea that "everything comes together" as personality, making each of us a predictable, recognizable, and rather intractable unity.

4. Fundamentally and above all else, we human beings are social creatures defined by our social roles, social interactions, and relationships. In this view, phenomena like "mob mentality," "authoritarian acquiescence," and "family conflict" reveal our true nature and discredit the lie that we are independent actors. In their different ways, family therapists and social therapists both champion this idea. For example, they see every "problem child" as a family problem. In this view, individual mental health is necessarily contextual and inseparable from family dynamics, group dynamics, interpersonal relationships, and

social life. Social psychology is the branch of
psychology most curious about these matters. Their
experiments are rather convincing in supporting the
idea that individuals are much more like herd animals
than people might like to imagine.

5. A view rather ignored by psychology and psychiatry is
    that we are embedded creatures whose circumstances
    matter much more than we are typically willing to
    admit. It matters if we must go to a school where we
    feel unsafe and are bullied mercilessly; it matters if we
    resent and don't like our mate; it matters if we must
    toil fifty hours a week at a menial or high-pressure
    job. In short, circumstances matter and dramatically
    affect our mental health. In this view, which I think
    strikes us as common sense, you would expect a
    homeless refugee to be "anxious" and "depressed," a
    marginalized youth to be "oppositional" and "defiant,"
    and so on. Any reasonable mental health model must
    naturally take a person's circumstances into account.

What these five views have in common is a rather stark failure
to picture human beings as possessing a real mind of the
sort that human beings actually have. These models on the
whole tend to not credit human beings with the ability to
chat with themselves about life, actively make sense of their
instincts, desires, psychological workings, and personality,
or realize that there are efforts they might make to help with
their sadness, anxiety, and other mental health challenges.
This is such an odd failure, really—to forget or ignore the fact
that human beings are able to chat with themselves about
what's going on.

There is a sixth view, then: we are dynamic, self-regulating
organisms that, to put it colloquially, can chat with ourselves
and aim ourselves in one direction versus another (for
example, toward calmness versus anxiousness, passion versus

indifference, love versus enmity, and so on). We may often do a poor job of dynamic self-regulation, indulging ourselves in thoughts and behaviors that don't serve us and actually preferring to think that we can't self-regulate. However, that's a shame and not an argument against the reality of self-regulation.

Human beings may be some impossible-to-deconstruct conglomeration of drives, appetites, thoughts, feelings, memories, neural events, and everything else human. But what we are *in addition* to all of that is a conscious being who knows things, understands things, and can try out things so as to help our situation improve. That's the premise of *Redesign Your Mind* and, I think, the truth of the matter.

Let's imagine how these six models might intersect. You are drinking too much. Your cells are adapting to your drinking habits and now crave alcohol. You certainly have a "biological" problem (you may have had a biological predisposition to begin with). Your mind likewise craves the alcohol, so you now have a "psychological issue" with respect to drinking. You also self-identify as a hard-drinking type and see drinking as a personality fit. Your "personality" helps sustain the problem. In addition, most of the adults in your family love to drink and you are caught up in a social dynamic that supports your drinking. On top of all that, your job is stressful and your marriage is on the rocks, so you drink to relieve those stresses. It's abundantly clear how all five—biology, psychology, personality, social pressures, and circumstances—contribute to your drinking problem.

But here's the human-sized miracle available to you: through dynamic self-regulation, simply by having a certain sort of chat with yourself, you can stop drinking from one minute to the next *despite the powerful nature of those five intersecting challenges*. You can enter into what is commonly called recovery, which is essentially an ongoing self-conversation about why you intend to not drink. There is a "you" that wants to drink, but there is also a "you" that knows better. That second "you" actively thinks, observes, reflects, counter-argues, and maintains an ongoing internal conversation in service of sobriety. Without that dynamic self-regulation piece, sobriety simply isn't happening. By virtue of it, sobriety is possible.

This is so important. *Those five are influential, but they're not determinative.* Isn't it to your great benefit to remember that this is possible and that the power of dynamic self-regulation is available to you? And really, isn't this the best way to picture a human being—not as a strictly biological creature, a strictly psychological creature, a strictly personality-defined creature, a strictly socially compelled creature, or a creature who is completely at the mercy of their circumstances, but rather, as a creature who, through self-conversation, can *figure things out*?

This view honors the reality of our capacity to think and constitutes our best path to mental health and emotional well-being. A dynamic self-regulation model of this sort does not reject the biological, psychological, personality, social, and circumstantial causes of mental and emotional distress. Rather, it rejects a reduced, inaccurate view of human beings as *just* their biology, psychology, personality, social interactions, or circumstances. A dynamic self-regulation model takes the most into account, and as a result, it provides you with the best chance of achieving mental health and emotional well-being.

· + ○ + ·

Visualization: See if you can visualize this thing I'm calling "dynamic self-regulation." You enter your mindroom and...what? What does dynamic self-regulation look like?

Writing Prompt: Pick an idea from Part I and think about it deeply.

REDESIGNING YOUR INDWELLING STYLE

LESS IMPULSIVENESS: PAUSING FOR SECOND ANSWERS

"The room that is your mind" is a metaphor. So is "indwelling style." Indwelling style is your characteristic way of being when you visit your mindroom: are you typically sad "in there," angry, critical, confused, etc.? Indwelling style also represents your mindroom's atmosphere: is it stuffy in there, claustrophobic, pressurized, etc.? Your indwelling style is the personality of your mindroom.

In Part II, we'll look at ways of transforming your indwelling style so that it better serves you. So far, we've looked at ideas like installing windows, substituting a bed of nails for an easy chair, and adding a safety valve. These ideas are easy to visualize. But what if you want to redesign how you *are* and how you *will operate* in your mindroom? That's a little harder to picture.

Consider the following. Something comes up and you really need an answer. Your mate receives a job offer to work on the other side of the world. Will you accompany them? You have a medical condition that might be treated in any one of three ways. Which treatment will you choose? At such times, do you settle down in your mindroom and think? Or when you go there, do you find a thought already waiting for you? "No, I'm not going!" "No, no chemo for me!" If you find a thought of that sort waiting for you—indeed, it pounces on you the moment you enter—how reliable should you consider it? And... *where did it even come from?*

I once spent a little time studying the reactions of French painters to the commencement of the Franco-Prussian War. The war began and each painter reacted idiosyncratically. One decided that it might prove valuable artistically to see war, and he therefore enlisted. A second shook his head at the madness of war and decided to ignore it completely. A third, wondering about his courage, enlisted to test himself. A fourth fled to the countryside to paint in peace and avoid conscription. A fifth protested the war. A sixth decided to stay home and paint "beautiful things" as a kind of antidote or counterpoint to the horribleness of war, using his parents' connections to avoid conscription. A seventh did nothing, got conscripted, and was killed almost immediately. And so on.

We understand each of these reactions. But more than that, we sense what has gone on in the mind of each of these painters. They heard about the commencement of hostilities and they reacted. An already-formed thought likely greeted each of them instantly, leaving no room for serious reflection. How many of these painters scoured all of their available choices and tried to decide which made the most sense? Probably none, don't you imagine? They reacted according to their formed personality, metaphorically snapping their fingers (hence the phrase "snap decision").

If an answer awaits as we walk in the door and some analysis, train of thought, or spontaneous reaction *has already taken place* before we even enter the room that is our mind, doesn't that enslave us to the murky doings of our unconscious and the straitjacket of our formed personality? And mustn't mastery of ourselves include an awareness that we will meet such already-formed answers with some skepticism, and that as powerful and influential as they feel, they must not be considered our final answer? They should only be the starting point of our inquiries. They are not gospel!

Remember that game show where a contestant would answer a question and the host would say, "Is that your final answer?" The contestant would pause and almost always repeat their answer, either because they were certain or because they had no better option than their chosen guess. For you, however, the answer that is waiting for you mustn't automatically be considered your final answer, since you haven't given the matter any real thought yet. When there is an important decision to be made, you want to think and not just react.

Since an automatic answer will likely be waiting for you, and since we are programmed to accept those answers, you will need to have a serious chat with yourself when you enter that room. Your chat might sound like: "I didn't arrive at this answer. It was just waiting for me. Since it was already waiting for me, it no doubt reflects some thoughts and feelings I'm having. But maybe it arose out of anxiety, fear, rage, or who knows what. Since it was waiting for me, that makes it too easy an answer and I therefore reject it. Instead of accepting it, I will think. If, upon reflection, I come to the same answer, then I'll trust it more. And if I come to a different answer—well then, thank goodness I checked!"

Doesn't this skepticism about the validity of ideas that are waiting for us throw the whole idea of intuition into question? It does and it should. Intuition, snap judgments, and snap decisions all have their place, but they are not to be revered above thinking, and they mustn't replace thinking when thinking is required. In retrospect, our life can look like a series of snap decisions. How well did that work out for you? You have a brilliant brain that would love to assist you, but don't accept its first answers. Make it do more work than that.

What does this look like as a visualization? At such times, when an important decision is required and an answer is already waiting for you, calmly turn on the lights, head to your easy chair, and *sit on your hands*. That gesture of sitting on your hands is the equivalent of you saying, "I am waiting to decide." By sitting on your hands, you temporize and give yourself a chance to really think. This will reduce your impulsiveness and help you make fewer wrong snap decisions. You won't send that email that you wish you hadn't sent the moment after you sent it. You won't say that thing to your mate that you wish you hadn't said the instant after you said it. Your easy chair serves many functions, one being that it is the place where you sit on your hands and think before you make important decisions.

· ✦ ○ ✦ ·

Visualization: Visualize yourself with a less impulsive indwelling style, one where calmness is the watchword and where, by virtue of you sitting on your hands, you give yourself the chance to make thoughtful (rather than impulsive) decisions.

Writing Prompt: If you have a history of impulsive decision-making, where does that impulsiveness come from? What's its source? See if you can dissect it a bit.

LESS SELF-SABOTAGE: ADMONISHING TRICKSTER

Human beings are very tricky creatures. We are tricky toward others and tricky toward ourselves. Why we might trick others is a little clearer: if we fool others, we may get what we want. But what do we get when we fool ourselves? What is the value of sabotaging ourselves? Whatever the reasons, many folks are burdened by an indwelling style characterized by self-sabotage. It's as if there's a mean trickster in there, one that we'd better admonish and try to exorcise—the goal of this chapter.

The trickster is a character out of world folklore. Cultures everywhere have identified this part of our nature. Let's foul the well water. Let's sleep with our neighbor's wife. Let's steal those chickens. Let's do worse. Let's plunder. Let's turn whole communities against one another. Let's make a giant mess of everyone's lives. Let's be a trickster!

Where do these sly, nasty, horrible impulses come from that inhabit everyone? Why is each of us such a trickster? Why do we start the day moral, compassionate, and upright, and somewhere around noon, turn into a coyote that's ravenous for mischief? Did the world offend us so deeply that we constantly ache for revenge? Did we not get our bottles on time as infants? What made us tricksters?

I vividly remember my own trickster moments from childhood. Two boys were racing side-by-side in the schoolyard, and out from the crowd lined up on either side came a foot to trip one of them—my foot. Why? I had nothing against the boy I tripped. I cared nothing about the outcome of the race. In fact, not a thing about those two boys racing mattered to me. So why spoil it for one of them?

In folklore, the trickster steals food, sex, fire, whatever he can. He changes shape so that he can't be spotted or caught. Is trickster sitting in a corner of your mind right now, maybe posing as a designer lamp, or a postcard from Spain, or a half-eaten sandwich? The second you blink, there he is: full coyote, wild-eyed, meaner than you imagined. Your very own trickster sub-personality, part of you, is hungry to damage someone—maybe you. In the room that is your mind, trickster is always around somewhere. Just lift up a corner of the rug or move a can of peas on the shelf. There's trickster!

What can be done to rid your mind of your trickster impulses? Can trickster be caged? Jailed? Banished? Tricked? No, none of that will work. But he can be admonished. You can wag your finger at that part of your nature and say, "That is absolutely not okay, that bit of mischief you're planning." Every time you see trickster, even if he's disguised as half of a tuna fish sandwich, you can exclaim, "Absolutely not, trickster. Absolutely not."

You can announce out loud, in that voice you use when you really mean something, that you are onto his tricks, that he isn't the least bit amusing, and that you really, really don't appreciate him. Don't give him an inch—he'll take your whole leg and your whole arm. Don't bestow even the smallest smile on him—he'll take that for full license. He is not your friend. He's devious and he wants to pull the wool over your eyes. Tell him you know what he's up to!

The room that is our mind is full of shadows. Pulling back the shades and letting in light can help. Turning on a lamp can help. We need more illumination and fewer shadows, more awareness and less impulsiveness. Where do those sly, nasty, downright vicious impulses come from? Who knows! Where do they reside? Right next to us as we read a book, right beside us in bed, right in our mind even as we try to be our civilized best. Trickster must be admonished. Maybe, just maybe, if we scold him often enough, he will leave. Maybe, finally, we can get rid of him.

Visualize that: visualize trickster leaving by the exit door you installed in Part I. Visualize him with his tail between his legs, leaving forever.

Trickster is not your friend. Trickster is no one's friend. His laugh is malicious, his plans are devious, and his desires are unworthy. We tolerate trickster living in our mind because, well, he is who we are. We are part-trickster. We are that bad boy and that bad girl. We are that person who would love to trip someone. We are that person who much prefers a stolen donut to a purchased one. Coyote lives in our mind because evolution invited him.

Right now, visit the room that is your mind and find trickster. He's somewhere—in the cupboard, in the corner, or sitting right in your own easy chair, laughing at you and daring you to move him. Find him and admonish him. Explain to him that you know him and that you do not cherish him. You do not find him funny and you do not want him living in your mind. It doesn't matter that he won't listen, that he'll play a game on you, that he'll change shape and become your socks, or that he can't be exterminated. Your job is to notice him and admonish him. Let him know—let you know, since you are trickster—that you do not admire him.

Visualization: Visualize yourself admonishing and defeating trickster. See him leave your mindroom. Visualize him gone!

Writing Prompt: Since trickster is part of our nature, it may feel strange to rid ourselves of him. Write on the prompt, "Can I live happily if I banish trickster, or am I going to miss his tricks?"

LESS DRAMA: DISPUTING TANTRUM MIND

Ever see a three-year-old throw a tantrum? Picture that three-year-old playing some obsessive game. All of their pieces are on the floor and in perfect order. They're consumed and in a trance, telling themselves a story about pirates or soldiers or train crashes. You walk by, friendly and amused, and accidentally knock one of their pieces off its mark. A quite amazing tantrum ensues, out of all proportion to that trifling accident.

It's absurd, really, considering that all that's required for perfect order to be restored is that they move that pirate or soldier or train back a few inches and put it in its place. Absurd or not, out of proportion or not, there it is: a real tantrum that no parent has yet figured out how to soothe or interrupt. That tantrum must just run its course.

That's really not so tragic, even if that tantrum happens in a supermarket and embarrasses you to no end. But what about its adult versions? Foreshadowed in that three-year-old's tantrum, don't we see road rage, domestic violence, family feuds, and war? In adults, the inability to forestall or interrupt a tantrum has massive effects. Whole mobs go into tantrum mode. Whole countries go into tantrum mode. And nothing known to man can stop them until the tantrum has run its course.

Versions of tantrum mind appear all the time in my coaching work with creative and performing artists. Here are four typical self-created dramas that I've encountered:

1. You're a writer. Someone you know says that they'll be happy to read your just-completed manuscript. You send them the manuscript. They reply that it turns out they are too busy to read your manuscript. From this relatively trivial event you create the most intense, dramatic, exclamation-point-littered drama about betrayal, humiliation, failure, and the essential cruelty of the universe. Why would a writer do that and derail themselves for six months, a year, or forever? Chalk it up to our human penchant for careless overdramatizing. Tantrum mind!

2. You're a painter. You've finished some new paintings and you're not sure what to charge for them. You have good reasons for charging what you usually charge (even for increasing your prices). At the same time, you could try charging almost any amount under the sun—from next to nothing to some outlandish amount— given the extraordinary range of prices for paintings. Rather than make some any choice, you turn this everyday difficulty into dramatic paralysis and stop selling and stop painting. You throw an internal tantrum, throw up your hands, and dive into despair. Tantrum mind!

3. You're a singer/songwriter. You've written some new songs and want to record them, but you're not sure which ones to record. This one sounds nicely commercial, but is it too commercial? This one is very artsy, but is it too quiet? This one is excellent but really requires an accompanist—who's available? This one is catchy, but doesn't it vaguely sound like somebody else's song? You stew about this and keep raising the

heat under the pot until the stew is boiling. Should it be this song, that song, or the other song? This song, that song, or the other song? Finally, the dramatic explosion that was coming arrives and you table your project indefinitely. Tantrum mind!

4. You're an actor. Your current headshots show you with short hair, but you think you look better with long hair, so you schedule a pretty expensive photo shoot. The day goes poorly, in part because you're not thrilled by the way you look, in part because the photographer doesn't seem sympathetic to your requests. You get the results of the photo shoot. Not one picture thrills you. Some are serviceable—but is serviceable good enough? You throw an internal fit about wasting all that money, about now having no headshots you like, and about the absurdity of the life you're leading. As a result, you avoid auditioning for the rest of the year. Tantrum mind!

We are all susceptible to these tantrums, and they make a bit of a mockery of the idea that we are capable of getting a grip on our mind or our emotions. But isn't there in fact a split second—the most micro of microseconds—during which time three-year-olds (and adults, too) allow themselves the indulgence of the tantrum? That briefest of brief moments that, as brief as it is, is nevertheless long enough for a three-year-old to say to themselves, "I think I'd like to throw a tantrum now. Here I go!"

Visualize *that* moment—that split second before you indulge yourself and throw a tantrum. It's only going to last a split second. Picture that moment...and freeze it!

I think we can change our mind in that split second. I think that we can dispute the impending tantrum. This would sound like: "I am not going to throw a tantrum now." Our mate may for the millionth time leave a dirty thing in the exact wrong place. We could throw a tantrum, or we could murmur, "I am not throwing a tantrum now." Are you justified in throwing that tantrum? Who can say. However, does it serve you to throw that tantrum? Almost certainly not. No three-year-old, after the fact and after some privilege has been withdrawn or some penalty exacted, has ever said to themselves, "That tantrum was *so* worth it." Nor has many an adult.

Sometimes we think, "A tantrum will feel so good!" But does it feel *that* good? This is a serious question. If tantrums actually made you happy, then that would amount to at least one reason to throw them—quite likely the only reason, since they never gain us anything or make a positive difference. But do they actually make you happy? Can you really say, "I'm so happy I threw that tantrum at work!" or "I'm so happy I threw that tantrum with my sister!" or "I'm so happy I threw that tantrum with that customer service representative!" Did any of those tantrums make you feel happy?

I think not.

Even if they did, even if those absurd, childish explosions provided relief that you experienced as pleasure, it would still be part of your program of dynamic self-regulation and healthy indwelling to put into practice a rejection of tantrums. You have an agenda—brilliant mental health—and you opt for that agenda to live your life-purpose choices and positively influence the creation of meaning in your life. Every tantrum, however good it may possibly feel, robs you of precious time and energy that you could be using to live well.

Experience tells us that even that three-year-old can gain some mastery over tantrums and can decide that, given the consequences of indulging those tantrums and given how bad they actually feel, they will stop themselves in their tracks.

They will not go wild when that pirate, soldier, or train is accidentally and unceremoniously moved. Many a three-year-old has come to that conclusion, and so can you.

You may not look like a drama queen or a drama king to the world, but something happens when you enter the room that is your mind. There, the moment you arrive, you are handed permission from yourself to throw a fit, upset all the furniture, and act as if your world has crashed into a million pieces. An engraved invitation was waiting and you accepted it. Why? Well, maybe life felt a little boring and you craved some excitement, even of this unfortunate kind. Maybe this was the straw that broke your back. Maybe you're furious about something else and this was a convenient trigger. Who can say? Whatever the reason for accepting it, you did.

Since this invitation is waiting for you, you'll need to prepare yourself for it right off the bat. First, pin a sign on the door to the room that is your mind: "No drama royalty allowed." Second, enter that room very carefully, watching out for invitations. If an invitation is thrust at you on a silver tray by a butler in livery, shake your head and murmur, "Ah, no, you've mistaken me for a diva." Third, stay alert as you move about. Some drama may be lurking behind the armoire or under the cushion of your easy chair, waiting to pounce.

Some part of us is inclined to exclaim at the drop of a hat, "The world has offended me!" If we were kings or queens, we'd lop off some heads. Not being royalty, we throw an internal tantrum. Wouldn't it be ever so much better to not play out that drama in the first place? Engrave on your easy chair, "This is not a throne." Put up little signs everywhere that say, "No dramas, please." Maybe that will make your room a little less exciting, but that's the wrong kind of excitement anyway.

Each of us has a tantrum mind—it's part of our inheritance. It's clear enough why nature thought that feature might serve us and why it would program our selfish genes to throw a really symphonic fit whenever we didn't get our way. But that genetic selfishness doesn't serve you or me. Let's do better, and in that microsecond before a tantrum is about to erupt, let's say "no" to it. That outburst you just prevented wasn't going to feel that delicious anyway. Spare yourself the loss of some essential self-worth and simply skip it.

· ✦ ○ ✦ ·

Visualization: Visualize your mindroom as a tantrum-free and drama-free zone. Remove anything, like a throne or crown jewels, that suggests you are royalty. Strategically place some signs: "No dramas, please," and "No tantrums, please."

Writing Prompt: Write on the question, "Why do I throw big fits over small matters?"

LESS CATASTROPHIZING: USING YOUR NON-MAGNIFYING GLASS

Our goal is to improve your indwelling style. So far, we've worked on becoming less impulsive, less self-sabotaging, and less dramatic. In this chapter, we're going to focus on what may be the unfortunate way that you magnify difficulty and how you find it hard to deal either with difficult thoughts or difficult circumstances.

Maybe there's some big thing that you know you need to do, like changing your job, separating from your mate, or stopping your drinking. This thing feels so huge, dangerous, and consequential that you can't get anywhere near tackling it. You think "I hate my job!" but then bite your lip, dismiss the thought, and proceed with your life.

A habit to learn is to tolerate such thoughts for more than a split second. Just that. Just practice tolerating a thought like "I need to begin dating again," or "I need a divorce," or "I need a new line of work." Notice the barrage of thoughts and feelings that assault you as you try to maintain that thought. Implore yourself to stay with the process.

Let's visualize that. Seat yourself comfortably in your easy chair, knowing that a hard moment is coming. See yourself there, in the safety of your redesigned mindroom, breathing, readying yourself to tolerate a thought that you know you don't want to be thinking. Use your safety valve to release the building pressure. Don't overdramatize the moment or begin to throw a tantrum of the "I shouldn't have to deal with all this!" sort. Be as calm as you can be, feel the wonderful ease of your easy chair, and think the thought. Keep breathing...

When and if you do try to hold a thought like "I need a divorce!" for several seconds, you're likely to be assaulted and bombarded by other thoughts like "If I leave him I'll suddenly be poor," "I've never worked a day in my life," "I'll feel like such a failure," "Children of divorce have so many problems," and "My parents will give me such a look when I tell them!" Try not to shut down. Try to keep tolerating the thought.

It may feel horribly hard. So many terrible potential consequences may flood your mind, but in order to make the changes that you need to make in life, the first step is to tolerate difficult thoughts. Don't worry about "doing anything" with the thoughts and feelings that flood you as you try to stay with that difficult thought. You don't have to dispute, answer, handle, accept, or do anything with them. You just have to survive them. You just have to tolerate them.

The activity of tolerating them creates calmness and an opening. You begin to see that you can survive the thoughts and feelings that come with thinking difficult thoughts. Decisions and action steps may come next. Whether they come or not, this is nevertheless the habit to learn: tolerate difficult thoughts. You've been setting up the room that is your mind to make it as safe and congenial a place as possible for thinking and feeling. Now picture it as a safe haven for tolerating difficult thoughts.

It will help if you get in the habit of not magnifying difficulties. We cause our own distress if we magnify the difficulty of our tasks. Our tasks are already real; there is no need to magnify them. Refusing to add incendiary language to our everyday self-talk is a vital habit to cultivate.

For example, if I was a painter and I said, "Let me call that gallery owner," I have added no unnecessary distress to an already charged task. If, however, I internally say, "Let me call that gallery owner. But where did I put that number? I'll probably get his answering machine, and then what will I say? But what if I get a person, what would I say *then*? I'm not sure I really want that gallery, but if I don't get it I won't be represented anywhere, and that means I will have no career whatsoever!" I have worked myself up and made it much more likely that I won't make that call. If I do manage to call, I'll likely handle the call poorly, having agitated myself so much.

Why do we magnify our difficulties in these ways? We do so for all sorts of understandable reasons. Maybe it's just the way our anxiety manifests. Maybe our tasks feel that difficult. Maybe it pleases us to see ourselves burdened by the sort of difficulties that only a warrior or hero could meet. Then, when and if we manage to handle them, we boost our ego. Maybe there is some emotional payoff to feeling victimized, beleaguered, or put-upon. Maybe life feels boring and we crave the dramas that we create when we pour fuel on what are small fires. These are common, completely human reasons for engaging in a practice that fails to serve us.

Begin to practice the habit of not magnifying difficulties. You do not need to shrink difficulties and act as if they do not exist. Just don't magnify them. How? By possessing a magnifying glass that does not magnify objects—it simply allows you to see what is there. Imagine how an ant would look through that sort of non-magnifying glass. It would look ant-sized. Imagine how an everyday task would look. It would look task-sized.

Visualize a small table next to your easy chair upon which you keep your non-magnifying glass. Use it to look at "life as it is," without magnifying difficulties.

The themes of this chapter are that it's hard to tolerate difficult thoughts and that tolerating them takes practice. It helps to tolerate them by learning not to magnify difficulties. Bringing up difficult thoughts creates whirlwinds and hurricanes, but it's important that you learn to bravely weather those storms. One key is to maintain a proper perspective by employing your handy non-magnifying glass.

· ✦ ◯ ✦ ·

Visualization: Picture yourself in your easy chair, looking at life clearly through your non-magnifying glass.

Writing Prompt: How might you go about doing a better job of distinguishing between a real difficulty and a magnified difficulty?

LESS EXISTENTIAL SADNESS: REMOVING YOUR HEAVY OVERCOAT

You and I regularly get sad. All human beings do. We get sad for all sorts of reasons, including two overlooked ones: that we may be born with a susceptibility to sadness, and that we may have trouble creating talking points that help us keep meaning afloat.

Because human beings get sad for all sorts of reasons, it may be the case that your experience of your mindroom is one dominated by sadness. It may be that you indwell as if you were wearing a heavy winter overcoat. In which case...let's take it off.

Of course, that is much easier said than done. One gift to give yourself that may allow you to actually remove that heavy winter overcoat is to pester yourself less about meaning. This is such an important idea. Once you begin to understand that it is rather a matter of luck if your efforts at making meaning actually provide the psychological experience of meaning, you can breathe, sigh, relax, and put meaning in its place.

It is such a heavy burden, after all, to *need* life to feel meaningful—for instance, to need the experience of writing your novel or running your lab experiment to feel meaningful as you are writing it or running it. The less you need life to feel meaningful, the less sadness you'll experience.

Let this idea sink in a little.

On top of the actual work required to live the project that is our life, must we also add to that burden the need for our efforts to feel meaningful? Isn't just living our life-purpose choices arduous enough? But no—we burden life with the added demand that it must feel meaningful. If it doesn't, we grow sad.

The answer is to get much more relaxed in the territory of meaning. Do not demand of experiences that they feel meaningful. Remove that winter overcoat and live your life-purpose choices in your shirtsleeves! As soon as you burden an experience with the need to feel meaningful, you're likely to have reduced its ability to provide that psychological experience. You'll have inadvertently slipped your overcoat back on. Do not burden experiences that way!

Let me clarify this idea a little. Let's say that you begin writing a novel because it wells up in you to write one. At the split second of beginning it, you're not thinking about whether or not writing it is going to prove meaningful—you just want to start writing it. By not putting any "meaning demands" on the experience, you're that much more likely to be provided with the psychological experience of meaning (at least for the first few moments, until the natural difficulties of process set in). You needed nothing from the experience of writing it, you only wanted to write. As a result, writing it is likely to prove meaningful, at least for a moment or two.

But say that you start the writing process from another place. Say that you are hungry for meaning and you make the conscious decision that writing a novel will constitute one of your meaning-making activities. You fully expect that working on it will provide you with the psychological experience of meaning. Now (ironically enough) you may find yourself *less likely* to experience meaning. A self-conscious demand on an activity to *feel meaningful* is likely to reduce its chances of actually feeling meaningful.

This may all sound a bit strange and new to you, talking about meaning in this way, as a certain sort of psychological experience about which you ought to concern yourself less. But I hope that the following idea does sink in: *you do not want to burden your efforts with the demand that they feel meaningful.* You can cherish the *hope* that something will provide you with the experience of meaning without attaching to it the *need* to provide you with that experience.

As an analogy, you can *hope* that the vacation you are about to take will prove enjoyable, maybe by virtue of all of the sunbathing you intend to get done, without *needing* the vacation to prove enjoyable. Then, if it happens to rain every day while you are there, you may still be able to enjoy your vacation because you weren't that attached to sunbathing or even to a need for joy. Likewise, you can *hope* that a given opportunity produces the experience of meaning without attaching a *need* for it to produce that experience.

You can't force life to mean, and you don't want to try to force life to mean either. Rather, you want to make conscious decisions about what efforts you think amount to value-based, meaning-making efforts that support your life-purpose choices—and then you want to *relax*. This deep relaxation is a philosophical stance that translates to: "I choose to do this next thing because I see it as valuable, whether or not it provides me with the experience of meaning."

To support this wise stance, visit the room that is your mind and remove your heavy overcoat. Install a closet, open it, select a sturdy hangar, and hang up that burdensome winter overcoat. Good riddance to it! With that gesture, you are signaling that you have gotten really easy with the whole "meaning" thing.

This is what "making meaning" entails: you value, you choose, you do, and then whatever happens, happens. As a result, you experience a sense of pride at having chosen, valued, and done something, even if you don't happen to experience meaning from the activity itself. And if you do experience meaning, that's something to celebrate!

Point yourself in the direction of your life-purpose choices, make the requisite effort, and then relax. If you do, that heavy overcoat will come flying off!

· ✦ ○ ✦ ·

Visualization: Visualize two things at once: yourself no longer needing experiences to feel meaningful, and that heavy winter overcoat slipping right off you. Visualize yourself in your shirtsleeves, finally easy with that whole "meaning" thing.

Writing Prompt: Consider and write about the idea that it is more important to live one's life purposes than to chase the experience of meaning.

LESS BOREDOM: YOUR BOREDOM REMINDER CARDS

There you are in the room that is your mind, sitting there... bored. That is a big problem.

Boredom breeds mischief, and that mischief (which can produce real messes) only relieves the boredom for a moment. You drive at a hundred miles an hour, but as soon as you park, the boredom returns. You engage in the wildest sex, but two seconds after orgasm, the boredom returns. Said the nineteenth-century novelist Stendhal:

> "This is the curse of our age, that even the strangest aberrations are no cure for boredom."

Hasn't the problem gotten even worse in this age of trivia? What to do?

Visualize a small deck of boredom reminder cards. The deck holds just five cards—a small enough number that you can remember what's on them without having to create them in actuality. If, however, you find that you can't remember what's on them, then you can actually create this small deck of cards and keep it handy.

The instant you're bored, pull out your deck and remind yourself of the following five headlines:

- "Do not fear boredom." This reminds you that boredom is a psychological state and that it will pass. Experiencing a little boredom is no tragedy and no reason to overthrow your life. Call boredom uncomfortable or disconcerting, but it's not the end of the world. Maybe on this first card is the following quote from Bertrand Russell: "Boredom is a vital problem for the moralist, since at least half the sins of mankind are caused by the fear of it." You smile. No, you aren't obliged to overdramatize the moment just because boredom brings with it a whiff of the void.

- "Boredom isn't an indictment of life." Boredom is just a bit of a meaning shortfall, a mini-meaning crisis. As a student of meaning, you know that meaning comes and goes. That it has vanished for a bit is not very startling. You simply turn to your list of cherished life purposes (you've created that list, yes?) and decide where you want to make some meaning next. And who knows, maybe this bit of boredom is a necessary precursor to some excellent creative activity. Maybe on this card is the following lovely reminder from the artist Marianne Mathiasen: "I have noticed that after a day of boredom I get more creative, so perhaps our brain needs a rest from time to time." Hold boredom as a precursor to something positive rather than as a negative statement about life.

- "Boredom motivates me." On it are two helpful quotes. One is from the sculptor Anish Kapoor: "It's precisely in those moments when I don't know what to do, boredom drives one to try a host of possibilities [to] either get somewhere or not get anywhere." The second is from the artist Gustav Klimt: "Today I want to start working again in earnest—I'm looking forward to it because doing nothing does become rather boring after a while." You remember that working regularly and productively dispels boredom. You take this bit of boredom as a wonderful reminder that you had better return to your life purposes and the project of your life.

- "What is this boredom masking?" Is what's going on really boredom, or is this fit of boredom masking some other feeling like resentment or rage? On this card are the following two quotes. The first is from the theologian Paul Tillich: "Boredom is rage spread thin." The second is from the novelist G. K. Chesterton: "A yawn is a silent shout." If what you are feeling isn't really boredom but something very different, get *that* challenge named.

- "Becoming my best me." This reminds you that you may not yet be the person that you need to be in order to effectively handle psychological challenges like boredom. Indeed, maybe your formed personality habitually creates boredom, in which case you will want to employ your available personality to move in the direction of an improved you. On this card is a message from the philosopher Soren Kierkegaard: "Boredom is the root of all evil—the despairing refusal to be oneself." When you become your best self, boredom might just vanish as an issue. This card reminds you that the boredom you're experiencing may be your cry for a personality upgrade.

Whether you only visualize these cards or whether you actually create a small deck that you keep handy, make use of this idea to deal with boredom and with other challenges as well. Visualize or create a small "sadness deck," or "anxiety deck," or "addiction deck." The idea is simple: provide yourself, via a small deck of cards, with a few headlines that help remind you of how you intend to meet one or another of the challenges that you regularly face.

· + ○ + ·

Visualization: Visualize a small deck of "boredom cards" that you use to quickly and effectively deal with the experience of boredom.

Writing Prompt: What does boredom signify to you?

LESS REPETITION: CHANGING ONE WORD

It is a feature of our formed personality to keep repeating our thoughts ad nauseam. This forced repetition promotes emotional pain and prevents growth and healing. If your indwelling style is characterized by repetitive thinking that makes a tense and stale atmosphere, wouldn't it be lovely to make some changes?

In the well-known German novel *Billiards at Half-Past Nine* by Heinrich Böll, a character has the same lunch every day: cottage cheese sprinkled with paprika. He is not a very likeable character. He is stiff, unbending, and ultimately cruel. We sense how little diversity this character is willing to tolerate in life. His repetitive lunch is a warning sign to us all: limit yourself, follow the rules, do not dare deviate!

Repetition is a sign of limitation that can prove accidentally dangerous in other ways. A given repetition may simply be unhealthy for us. Someone I knew brought the same supposedly healthy lunch to work every day for years—a tuna fish sandwich—and became demented from all that mercury. He presumed that he was doing the right thing, but he wasn't. Changing his lunch routine would have saved him.

Repeating ourselves is fine, but a too-steady diet of the same thing can signal that we are living a small and straightjacketed life. Repetition can prove risky in our daily lives, and it's the same with our thoughts.

Say that you're thinking a thought that doesn't particularly serve you. Thinking it once is unfortunate. But thinking it a million times, hour after hour and day after day, hijacks your life. Just imagine thinking, "I have no chance," over and over again. Imagine "I have no chance" constantly blinking in green neon on the wall opposite your easy chair. How easy would that easy chair feel if you had to look at that malignant indictment every second? All day and all night: "I have no chance." You take a nap, wake up, and there it is again: "I have no chance." How would that sort of life feel?

There are serious things you can do to try to stop those caustic repetitions. But there are also amusing and rather goofy things to try. Here is an amusing and goofy one: simply change one word of the thought. Put in any new word you like. Instead of thinking "I have no chance," try "I have no socks," or "I have no celery," or "Goats have no chance." Silly, isn't it? But who's to say that silly can't also be brilliant?

Maybe the repetitive thought is "Nothing about life is fair." Change one word. "Nothing about paragliding is fair," or "Nothing about life is purple." Maybe the repetitive thought is "There's so much competition." Change one word. "There's so much shortcake," or "There's so much alfalfa." Does changing a word in this fashion make life fair or reduce the competition you face? No, it doesn't. But it may disrupt your pattern of self-talk, ending the trance you're in and allowing you to laugh just a little. Wouldn't that be something?

We know all about repetitive, unproductive, obsessive self-talk. We know how debilitating and damaging that self-talk can be. If we ask ourselves again and again, "Did I lock the door?" we wear ourselves out and kidnap neurons that might otherwise be used for good work. Isn't that the essence of mental staleness, boredom, and agitation? "Oh, my gosh, not that

thought again!" How tiring! How maddening! But there it is.
Given this terrible penchant for repeating ourselves, we need
as many tactics as we can muster to interrupt that onslaught.

These are exactly the sorts of tactics and strategies that
cognitive therapists regularly offer, tactics like thought
stopping and thought substituting. But rarely are their tactics
amusing or absurd-seeming. These cognitive therapists
are professionals, after all, with a professional demeanor to
uphold. It wouldn't do for them to present you with a silly
strategy. But silly might be just what the doctor ordered.
Imagine saying "I have no flies" rather than "I have no chance."
Don't you feel better already?

You might change a word because you want to make a point
to yourself (for example, changing "I have no chance" to
"I have some chance," or changing "Nothing about life is
fair" to "Lots about life is fair"). We would understand your
intention in each instance: you are wanting to paint a picture
of life as better. That makes perfect sense. But for my little
exercise, I would like you to be sillier than that and head in
the direction of nonsense. Pick words that make no contextual
sense and create sentences that are patently ridiculous. I am
trying to get you to smile! Please play along and see what
you experience.

Get yourself ready. When you think a thought that you know
doesn't serve you, say to yourself, "If I have that thought
again today, I'm changing one word and turning it goofy." If
that thought arrives a second time, smile, say it out loud—for
instance, "I have no chance"—and then say it again with a
word substituted. "I have no raisins." "I have no walnuts."
This may not get to the heart of the matter, but it may make
you giggle and provide you with a respite, and giggling and
respites are not nothing.

· + ○ + ·

Visualization: Visualize yourself sitting in your easy chair. You're not sure what you might like to think about, but you're certain that this same obsessive, repetitive thought isn't it. Visualize yourself repeating that thought with a word changed, turning it silly, smiling or even laughing a little, and getting on with some better thinking.

Writing Prompt: Pick one of your repetitive thoughts. Turn it silly twenty different ways. After doing that, see if you can even remember what the thought was!

LESS INCOMPLETION: USING YOUR COMPLETION CHECKLIST

Most people fail to complete what they begin. They try to start an online business but don't quite manage to do so. They begin to learn Chinese or how to play the guitar but stop almost immediately. In my work over the past thirty-five years coaching creative and performing artists, I see this all the time. Creatives often near the finish line on a project and then stop before completing it. Why does this happen so regularly? Here are five of many reasons, framed from the point of view of a painter:

1. The painting-in-progress doesn't match the artist's original vision for the piece. Very often an artist "sees" their painting before it's painted—all its beauty, grandeur, and excellence. And then, as they paint, the "real" painting in front of them doesn't match the brilliance and perfection of their original vision. Disappointed, they lose motivation to complete their creative project and either white-knuckle their way to the end or in fact don't complete it.

2. They fear that this is their best idea and that they may not have another excellent one ever again. The brain can fool you into thinking that your current idea is

the last excellent idea you'll ever have. You can get weighed down by thinking that since no other idea will ever come to you, you had better nurse this one. That gives you something to work on and puts off what you feel will be a terrible reckoning when this painting is done: facing the void and discovering that you have nothing left to say.

3. They fear losing their current good feelings. Say that you're currently doing a series of red paintings. All that red is making you feel buoyant and joyful. You have it in your mind that you will do a blue series next. While that makes sense to you intellectually and aesthetically, it doesn't move your heart that much. These red paintings feel wonderful; the coming blue ones feel a little cool, verging on cold. So as to keep this loving feeling alive, you decide just out of conscious awareness to not finish these red paintings. You just want a little more time with them, so you don't complete them.

4. They're not ready for the process to start all over again. Many artists find the start of each new work of art to be something of a trial, even a little traumatic. At the moment of needing to begin, they pester themselves with questions like "Do I have another good idea in me?" or "Am I really working in the right style?" or "Will this be just another one of my paintings that no one wants?" Many artists prefer to keep working on their current project, even if it is done or could readily be completed, rather than facing the unpleasant reality of another blank canvas.

5. The appraising will then have to begin. While you're working on a piece, you can keep saying to yourself, "Yes, maybe it isn't wonderful yet, but by the end it will be!" You hold out the carrot that your further efforts

will transform the work into something you really love. But once you say it is complete, then you actually have to appraise it and decide if it is or isn't excellent, or even any good. Because we want to put off that moment of reckoning, we are inclined to say, "Well, let me do just a little more." As a result, we continue to tinker, often ruining the work.

What can help with this problem of not completing your work? Keeping a pad of "completion checklists" in a drawer in your mindroom.

If you're building a house and you're approaching the end of the process, you know to create a punch list of last things that have to get done: spot painting, putting in a last light fixture, and so on. When you've completed everything on your punch list, you can be pretty certain that you are done. By contrast, a creative likely has no such checklist or punch list, would probably never dream of creating one, and even if the concept popped into their head, would probably have no idea what to put on such a list.

A literal completion checklist for each of your projects might prove really invaluable. But here, I'm suggesting just a visualization. Visualize yourself pulling out your pad of completion checklists, tearing off the top one, filling it out, and experiencing the sensation of *intending* to complete your current project. This visualization sets an intention. If you have a literal checklist, that's wonderful. But whether or not you have a literal one, you can use this visualization to remind yourself that you intend to finish and to remind yourself that finishing involves a significant number of concrete tasks. This visualization helps solidify what may be only a fleeting feeling: "I intend to finish, and sooner rather than later!"

· + ○ + ·

Visualization: Visualize a pad of completion checklists and visualize yourself actually using that pad to help set an intention to finish the projects you begin.

Writing Prompt: Is it your habit to not complete projects? Might visualizing intending to complete them—or actually completing them—help some?

LESS STARVATION: ENGAGING IN APPETITE ARTISTRY

Many people look to have too much appetite: cravings for alcohol, sweets, sex, gambling, internet diversions. But all that apparent appetite may actually be hunger in disguise.

If you're starving for meaning and purpose, you may well decide to fill up with Scotch, shopping, or online poker. If this is your way of dealing with that hunger, it would be wise to take that into account as you redesign your mindroom. Wouldn't it be lovely if there were a dedicated place in your mindroom where, the second you arrived, you got really hungry—not for food, drugs, or some diversion, but for something meaningful to bite into, like some idea, project, or activity? Some life-purpose choice?

If you don't possess such a place, you might end up like Kafka's titular hunger artist, who wasted away as a circus attraction because he could find no food that interested him. Kafka's hunger artist, that classic sad figure from existential literature who could fast so well, spent his days starving in front of amused customers who paid to see his slow demise. From his point of view, he possessed no particular skill. It was simply that no food had ever interested him. When asked by his supervisor how he'd acquired his "admirable talent" for fasting, the hunger artist replied:

" 'But you shouldn't admire it,' said the hunger artist... lifting his head a little and, with his lips pursed as if for a kiss, speaking right into the supervisor's ear so that he wouldn't miss anything, 'because I couldn't find a food which I enjoyed. If I had found that, believe me, I would not have made a spectacle of myself and would have eaten to my heart's content, like you and everyone else.' Those were his last words, but in his failing eyes there was the firm, if no longer proud, conviction that he was continuing to fast."

Many people find themselves in this odd situation: firm, but not proud, in their conviction that there is nothing in life that does or *can* genuinely interest them. They claim that they would dearly love it if something *did* passionately interest them, and yet their claim sounds just a little hollow, as hollow as the hunger artist's. Is it really the case that a person in decent health and in decent spirits can't find ice cream, pizza, barbecued ribs, or *something* tasty? Or is it rather that they are in poor spirits (existentially speaking), such that their appetite has been suppressed, even ruined?

Whatever the precise reasons for this malaise, countless smart, sensitive, creative people find themselves in the position of Kafka's hunger artist: wasting away, in love with nothing, and convinced that at second glance, all pursuits are bound to turn empty and meaningless. Nothing seems able to provoke the psychological experience of meaning in them. They read a novel, it was okay. Now what? They plant roses, that was okay. Now what? They learn carpentry, they make a few objects. Now what? They take a class, it was interesting enough. Now what? They start a business, the stress outweighs the rewards. On to the next thing.

A person who stands as a hobbyist in life, bereft of meaning, is bound to despair. Yet there is some odd stubbornness to their plight, too. It's as if they are determined to not give up their worldview, even if another one might come with meaning, just as addicts fiercely hold on to their addictions and only pay lip service—or no service at all—to the idea of recovery and a life without their cigarettes, cocaine, or alcohol. Many smart, sensitive, creative people become attached to both a life empty of meaning and this strange addiction: their stubborn refusal to take a genuine stab at making meaning.

A great many folks entertain enthusiasms, hobbies, and interests, pursue an education and then a career, and so on, and yet never land on anything—a subject, a line of work, a life—that they feel passionate about. Even their enthusiasms, hobbies, and interests bore them in short order. Here's how Sandra, a client of mine, described her situation:

> "At forty-nine, I find that I have not been able to sustain interest in anything really. Art in the broadest sense is the closest thing. I like it all, but nothing really sticks. There's nothing that I'm specifically passionate about, but I wish there was. I can't help but feel that if I concentrate on one activity, I'll be missing out on another. Am I just greedy? Do I have the passion but not the focus? I envy artists who can explore their subjects in depth over time. It feels like I will live my whole life trying to decide what I want to be when I grow up."

No doubt each hunger artist became a hunger artist in their own way. There is no single path to a lifetime of acute meaninglessness. There are so many ways to kill off meaning:

not caring, not committing, not finding the courage, not choosing, not besting demons, not standing up, declaring that life is a cheat. One answer? Make sure that there is a place in your mindroom—a certain chair, a certain corner, a certain nook—where, the instant that you arrive there, you feel ravenous.

Visualize that right now. Visualize yourself in your mindroom, seated or standing, ravenous for life and not for life substitutes. Feel that? See that? Are you ravenous now? Good! See yourself indwelling that way and visualize the consequences. What would happen next?

· ✦ ○ ✦ ·

Visualization: Visualize yourself in your mindroom, eager to identify your life purposes, eager to make meaning, ravenous to live!

Writing Prompt: Discuss how something like overeating (or whatever addiction attracts you) might be less an appetite for food and more a lack of appetite for life.

LESS NEGATIVITY: WALKING BY THE RIVER

Your indwelling style maters. Likewise, how you evaluate life matters. You experience life against the backdrop of your evaluation of it, and if your evaluation of life is negative, nothing has much of a chance of feeling positive. What if you've gone so far as to evaluate life as a complete cheat? Isn't that evaluation bound to promote chronic sadness?

Why might you have evaluated life that harshly? Maybe it's because you went unloved as a child. Maybe it's because you spend a stupendous amount of time just earning a living. Maybe it's because you never met your soul mate. Maybe it's because you see immorality rewarded and good deeds punished. Maybe it's because you had dreams that never materialized and goals that you never met. Maybe it's because you see clearly how money is unfairly distributed. Maybe it's because you just expected *more* out of life—more from it, more from others, more from yourself. Indeed, doesn't it seem rather fairer to evaluate life as a cheat rather than as something worth the candle?

However, a great many people have evaluated life as a cheat without realizing that they made this decision, and without realizing how many unfortunate consequences flow from this decision. You may be one of these many. If you are, you may have ample reasons to conclude that life is a cheat, but you will feel better if you decide nevertheless that life is worth living. It is in your best interest to decide that life matters.

Can you manage to evaluate life in a positive way even though you've been badly disappointed in the past, and even though you find life taxing and unrewarding? That is a conversation that you really ought to have with yourself. Visit the room that is your mind, settle into your easy chair, enjoy the warmth of the fire blazing in the fireplace opposite, and ask yourself this hard question: "Could it be that I've evaluated life as a cheat?" If the answer is "yes" or "maybe," ask this follow-up question: "What can I do to change my mind and give life a thumbs-up, even if life doesn't quite deserve it?"

Please ask and try to answer these questions.

Maybe your easy chair isn't quite the place for this conversation. If it turns out not be, let's design a special place in your mindroom for these important, difficult conversations. Maybe outside would be even better. Maybe you'd be better off having this conversation while taking a stroll. In that case, let's add a shady path by the river right out the back door of your mindroom. Leave your mindroom without leaving it, saunter by the river, be one with the birds and the flowers, enjoy the loveliness of a summer's day, and chat with yourself about how exactly you're going to go about giving life a thumbs-up.

Because we human beings wall off knowledge that upsets us, we may not know that we have evaluated life as pointless, a cheat, and a fraud. It might be expected that we would get some clues from our behaviors—that we drink a lot, take antidepressants, fantasize about taking revenge. But we may find it just too painful to announce the cause of our suffering: that we have evaluated life negatively. A great many people, maybe even the vast majority, have come to negative conclusions and evaluations about life but deny that they have given life a thumbs-down.

If you agree with me that how you evaluate life colors how you experience it, provides or fails to provide you with motivational juice, and largely determines whether or not you will live according to your principles, then you are obliged to attempt the odd work of thoughtfully deciding to evaluate life more positively. Maybe, just maybe, you can. Maybe you can come down on the side of affirming that life matters.

If you manage to paint this different sort of picture for yourself—one that conceptualizes life not as a cheat and a fraud but as a project, an obligation, an opportunity to make yourself proud, and even as an adventure—you will discover that you experience meaning more often and that those experiences of meaning begin to accumulate and count. Meaninglessness may even begin to recede as an issue!

Go your mindroom right now and have this conversation. Maybe you'll have it sitting in your easy chair, maybe walking by the river will suit you better. Whatever way you decide to design your experience, it's time to deal with the possibility that your negative evaluation of life may be dragging you down. Indeed, your very way of indwelling may be held hostage by that negativity. Don't let your mindroom be a negative place where you are always shaking your head. Find the way to nod and affirm life.

· ✦ ○ ✦ ·

Visualization: Visualize yourself giving life a robust thumbs-up, even if you have many reasons to evaluate it negatively.

Writing Prompt: Have you secretly evaluated life as a cheat? What are your thoughts on that?

LESS RESISTANCE: RELEASING ICE CUBES

Let's say that you're a creative person. Like many creatives, you may find yourself regularly resisting doing your creative and intellectual work. Why? There are lots of potential reasons, like:

- Maybe the work is arduous.
- Maybe the work is disappointing you.
- Maybe the work is proving deathly boring.
- Maybe you have hard choices to make, say, about where to take the plot of your novel.
- Maybe your to-do list of chores and responsibilities is making itself felt and demanding your attention.
- Maybe you're feeling like your current project is too much like something you did before.

Even if everything seems just fine, we can still feel resistant to sitting down and getting started. Often it seems as if there's a thin layer of ice between us and our creative work, a layer of resistance that we have to forcibly crack through, sometimes on a daily basis.

What can help? Well, cracking through that ice!

You know that cracking sound that a twistable ice cube tray makes when you twist it and loosen the ice cubes? That's a sound most of us know well. Let's make use of that knowledge. Stock your mindroom with a small refrigerator with a tiny freezer compartment just big enough to hold a single plastic tray of ice cubes. You can use the refrigerated section to keep the most expensive treats in the world (since you don't actually have to buy them), or as a place where you store your homelier goodies—maybe your daily cucumber and carrot snack. But reserve the freezer section for your resistance-busting ice cube tray.

How might you use your ice cube tray? You might ceremonially go to your mindroom refrigerator every day just before your daily creative stint, open the freezer compartment, remove the ice cube tray, and give it a mighty twist. What a great cracking noise you'll make! Experience your resistance cracking as that ice cracks. Quickly put the ice cube tray back—no need to refill it, as you haven't actually used any of the ice cubes you loosened—and hurry off to begin your creative work.

You might reserve this exercise for times when you feel particularly stuck and unmotivated. A day passes without creating, then two days pass. In the blink of eye, a month has vanished. You know that you had better do something, and now you know exactly what to do. Crack some ice!

In case twisting an ice cube tray doesn't produce the result you want, try a different mind ceremony. You might envision cracking an egg against the side of a bowl. You might envision walking out onto a lake on a bright winter's day and feeling the ice cracking under your feet. You might envision smashing a vase against the wall. You might envision hearing the crack of a pitched ball hit with a baseball bat. In your mind's eye, you can try out anything! Create a variety of cracking exercises and give each one a try. Maybe you'll land on one that becomes your go-to resistance buster.

Many creatives suffer from the anxiety state called perfectionism. Their fear of imperfection causes them to refuse to create until they've acquired some internal guarantee that what they're about to create will prove excellent. But the realities of the creative process preclude such guarantees. As a result, they wait and wait and maybe never begin. Cracking something in your mind's eye—an egg, a sheet of ice, a glass rendering of the word "perfect"—can help with this sort of long-standing block. It's certainly worth a try!

Creating just the right cracking experience will help you break through everyday resistance and dissolve long-standing blocks. Few things are as disappointing as not getting to your creative work. It may be just the thinnest veneer of ice that stands between you and your work, and all that is needed is a gentle tap—maybe a good rap—in order to crack through. Twist that ice cube tray, hear that wonderful crack sound, and get on with your work.

· ✦ ⭘ ✦ ·

Visualization: Visualize twisting a plastic ice cube tray, releasing its contents with a mighty cracking sound, and breaking through the resistance that's keeping you from your work.

Writing Prompt: Have a discussion with yourself about what you intend to do when you feel blocked or resistant.

LESS FEAR: EMBRACING AN OLD FRIEND

All of the thinking that we need to do—from calculating, to problem-solving, to predicting, to creating—produces a certain amount of anxiety.

This natural anxiety might be handled relatively easily if we just remembered that it was coming, and if we possessed some anxiety management techniques to deal with it. Our usual way, however, is to not see the anxiety coming. We have no good plan in place to deal with it, are surprised each time it arrives, and instead of handling it well, we employ one of the following unfortunate anxiety reduction methods:

- Maybe we flee the encounter—that is, we run away from the activity of thinking. We begin to think about something we need to think about, and almost immediately get up and do something else. Or we stay put but send our mind elsewhere, somewhere easier on our nervous system, like off to shop, play a game, or check the weather.

- Maybe we employ some dangerous "canalizing" tactic, so as to help ourselves stay put. We scratch at our head until it bleeds, we bite our fingernails until they're bitten down, we keep a Scotch bottle or a pack of cigarettes handy or soothe ourselves in some other unhelpful way as we struggle to think.

- Maybe we quickly opt to think small. Maybe we have a certain novel in mind to write. We sit down to begin it, anxiety wells up in us, and we decide to write a blog post instead. Writing that blog post allows us to congratulate ourselves on having gotten *something* done. But inevitably, those congratulations turn to chagrin, since a part of us knows what our real intention was when we sat down.

- Maybe we play it safe in other ways. For instance, it is much easier on the brain to repeat a memorized message than to think. Most people who regularly communicate with others do not do much thinking on their feet, as that is anxiety-provoking work. Instead, they craft messages and then repeat them. Those repeated messages are then woven into a stump speech or become the tapes that they run. We sound more intelligent and more confident and do a better job of staying on point when we just repeat our canned messages. But where's the creativity, innovation, or heart in that?

- Maybe we instantly fantasize. As soon as that anxiety arrives, a smart person who naturally loves story, metaphor, narrative, and fantasy can easily stop working on their novel and instead fantasize about winning the Nobel Prize. They let their mind wander, fantasizing about success, conquests, revenge, or anything else that might prove soothing and distracting. Because the brain of a creative person is agile, it can spin itself lovely fantasies all day long—winning a battle with ferocious creatures in the morning, winning love at midday, and winning a Pulitzer in the evening. But fantasizing doesn't get diseases cured or novels written.

- Maybe we over-prepare ourselves by doing a little more researching, or by leaving our work to read another book or attend another lecture. In a corner of awareness, we likely know the exact game we're playing, which further distresses us, disappoints us, and raises our anxiety level. Or maybe we try to circumvent the process. We might well wish that the process was different, and if we do wish that, we may find ourselves attracted to seminars on "the ten tricks for mistake-free thinking," or "the secret to perfect thinking." But what we are actually doing is avoiding the process, avoiding the anxiety, and avoiding doing the thinking.

John, a coaching client and a medical researcher, explained to me:

"I use all of these methods! I had no idea that my cigarette smoking, my procrastinating, my fantasizing, my reading yet another journal article, my opting to toil in a tiny corner of my field, are all connected at this base level, as ways to avoid the anxiety of thinking. Now I see exactly how they connect! I have to face the fact that aiming my brain at a difficult research question and tackling that question are going to make me anxious—period. I have to embrace that truth...and deal with it!"

The anxiety is surely coming. Visualize it coming. Now, here's the switch to make. Do not picture it as a monster. Visualize it as an old friend and embrace it as such.

Yes, of course you'd prefer that your old friend not visit. Yes, they aren't really a friend. But they aren't a stranger, either, or an enemy. They're a feature of your early warning system, alerting you to inchoate danger. As that is their evolutionary function, they are not our enemy. Greet them and learn to manage them effectively. There are scores of techniques to try: breathing techniques, cognitive techniques, relaxation techniques, stress-discharge techniques, reorienting techniques, disidentification techniques, and many more. Learn what to do when your old friend anxiety visits.

There you are, sitting in your easy chair in the room that is your mind, thinking hard about something. You notice some anxiety welling up. This no longer surprises you—now you know better than to be surprised. You murmur, "Hello, old friend." You smile a little. You rather expected their visit. You know that they can't be barred from the room that is your mind and you've learned (or are learning) how to make their visit as short as possible.

· ✢ ○ ✢ ·

Visualization: Visualize yourself dealing with the anxiety that is going to inevitably arise sometimes by embracing that anxiety as if it were an old friend. Visualize that embrace. Feel how that embrace brings instant ease and calm.

Writing Prompt: Write on the prompt, "What do I currently do when I try to think about something and suddenly feel anxious?"

SILENCED SALLY

Indwelling, the subject of Part II, is a deep reservoir subject, full of twists, turns, and human intricacies. In this chapter and the next, we'll examine some of these intricacies as we look a pair of my clients. First up is Sally.

· + ○ + ·

When I worked as a psychotherapist, Sally came to see me. Sally worked in the nonprofit world as a fundraiser, had three grown children and a demanding husband, and presented herself to the world as a cheerful person. But she recognized that she was extremely anxious and sad much of time. She came to me feeling hopeless and helpless.

Anxiety and sadness are, of course, not necessarily related. We can experience anxiety whether or not we are also experiencing something else, like sadness. Anxiety is a feature of our danger warning system, and as such, it is independent of any particular feeling. We may be feeling happy, say, while at a party. Then something or someone threatens us and suddenly we're highly anxious. Anxiety connects to threat.

But if we are also regularly sad, that opens the door to anxiety. And if we are regularly anxious, that likewise opens the door to sadness. It's simple to understand why. It is going to make us feel sad that we are so burdened by anxiety, and it is going to make us more anxious if we are looking out at the world from a place of sadness. Those connections are easy to see.

Therefore, it might seem straightforward to say, "Reduce your anxiety and that will reduce your sadness." But life isn't that straightforward. Sometimes we have to do something that *increases* our anxiety in order to reduce our sadness. That was Sally's situation.

Sally had no trouble speaking. She was a verbal woman who managed people in her day job and who got things done. But she had terrible trouble saying what was *really* on her mind when it came to dealing with her husband, her adult children, her aging parents, her siblings, and everyone else in her family. With them, she said cheerful, upbeat, noncritical, nonthreatening things...and experienced herself getting trampled by them.

This, of course, made her sad. We broached the idea that maybe one of our goals would be not to focus on reducing her anxiety, but rather to focus on her speaking up, even if that increased her anxiety. Until she spoke up, it was very hard to see how the sadness she was experiencing could possibly be reduced. We picked one particular issue—a kitchen remodel— and rehearsed her telling her husband what she really wanted to say to him. This practicing, rehearsing, and preparing took several weeks.

Finally, she confronted him. The conversation went exactly as poorly as she predicted it would. But she spoke her mind. That was of paramount importance. And although it did in fact increase her anxiety because she was now in conflict with her husband, she also felt *less* anxious because she saw that she could survive speaking. She felt simultaneously more and less anxious, which is so very human. We had to laugh: how could a person feel more and less anxious at exactly the same moment? But Sally did. And most importantly, she also felt less sad. She felt rather invigorated...and ready to say more.

There may be something you need to do that (initially, at least) may raise your anxiety level, but that will ultimately release your sadness. Is there some such thing? Let's engage with that visualization. Enter your mindroom. Flip the light switch that doubles as your calmness switch. Feel the relief. Open a window. Let in a summer breeze. Take a look at the gauge next to your pressure release valve: how's the pressure? Mounting? If so, use your release valve to lower it. Hear the hiss of that pressure escaping.

Move to your easy chair. Think about the thing you need to do to release your sadness. If thinking that thought increases your anxiety, leave by the exit door and take a walk by the river. Do your best to tolerate that hard thought as you walk among the birds and the bees and the flowers. Return to your mindroom and set your intention. Visualize yourself doing the thing that you know you need to do to release your sadness. Maybe it's speaking up, maybe it's giving life a real thumbs-up gesture, maybe it's finally dealing with your self-sabotaging trickster. Stay steady as you visualize yourself doing that thing.

Can you see how you are changing and improving your indwelling style when you start to operate and live your life like this?

· ✦ ○ ✦ ·

Visualization: Visualize yourself taking the steps to make it easier for you to tolerate thinking about the thing that you know you need to think about. Then visualize yourself thinking that difficult thought. Then visualize yourself following through with the action that matches your newly formed intention.

Writing Prompt: What are you learning about indwelling? Spend a little time getting down your thoughts about what "indwelling style" is beginning to mean to you.

ENRAGED BILL

You are redesigning your mind so as to make it a more congenial, productive, and self-friendly place. You are also redesigning it so as to increase your self-awareness. Many people go a lifetime without ever understanding what they are really feeling or what is really motivating their behaviors. To take one example: it is entirely possible to be sad your whole life without ever actually feeling sad. That sounds like a paradox, doesn't it? Like a play on words, a riddle, or just plain preposterous, but consider it.

When I worked as a psychotherapist, one of my clients was an Army vet by the name of Bill. Bill was strong, tough, and had an edge to him. He worked as a security guard by day and drummed in a heavy metal band by night. He came to see me about what he'd labelled his post-traumatic stress disorder.

"You were in Iraq?" I asked.

"Yes. Two tours."

"You had terrible experiences there?"

"Yes."

"Let's go back in time a little, let's say to high school. How were you back then?"

"I was on the football team," he said. "So I was kind of into teamwork. But I didn't really get on with anyone."

"And were you happy? Sad? What?"

"I was angry. I was angry all the time."

"At?"

Bill shrugged. "My father. I hated my father. And my mother. She was worse than my father. I hated everybody, really. And everything."

I nodded. "I always like to check in on sadness. Were you sad growing up?"

Bill frowned. "Not that I remember."

"No?"

"You mean depressed?"

"No. I'm just using simple language here. You know, sad versus happy."

"Well, I was never happy."

I smiled. "Well, that doesn't necessarily mean that you were sad. Those aren't the only two possibilities. You could have been, well, kind of neutral. Neither sad nor happy."

Bill thought about that. "If you'd looked at me, you'd have said that I was angry. You'd have experienced me that way. A short fuse. A ticking time bomb. I wasn't happy and I wasn't sad. I was angry."

I could tell that he wasn't finished. "And?" I asked after a moment.

"Underneath? How to put this...I think that I would have been sad if I'd had permission to be sad."

"Permission from?"

"My father, first of all. But then, ultimately myself. I would have been very sad if I hadn't stopped myself from being sad. Sad wasn't something I could be. I could be angry. That I allowed myself. That I even relished, if that's the word. But I couldn't allow myself to feel sad."

"Because?"

He shrugged again. "Because that would have been admitting that they'd hurt me. I could hate them for hurting me, but I couldn't admit that they'd hurt me."

153

"The way your Army experiences have hurt you?"

"Yes," he said after a moment.

I nodded. "So you weren't sad because you didn't have permission to be sad. But if you'd somehow had that permission, you would have been sad?"

"Yes. All the time."

We sat together in silence.

"Is it fair to say," I continued, "that you were sad all the time even though you were never sad?"

Bill nodded. "That's exactly the way it was."

Think about your own life. Have you had an experience like Bill's? Have you experienced some emotion like rage, boredom, restlessness, recklessness, or something else, because you didn't have permission to feel sad? Maybe you were born sad, or born ready to become sad, and never actually experienced that sadness because you had no permission to do so. To have let yourself feel sad would have been to admit too much and to feel too much.

How would you like to redesign your mind so that information of this sort becomes available to you? We're talking about you gaining permission to think thoughts, feel feelings, and learn things about yourself that you've previously kept walled off from your conscious awareness. Might visualizing knocking down a wall help? You know those home improvement shows where the new owners want an "open concept" floor plan and merrily knock down walls on demolition day? Might a demolition day serve you? Give that some thought.

Visualization: Visualize yourself knocking down a wall in your mindroom and allowing new information to flood in. Get ready for that flood of information!

Writing Prompt: Do you think that there might be some important self-knowledge just out of conscious awareness that it's time to notice? If so… what is it?

THE LOOK OF UNHEALTHY INDWELLING

Let's take a look at how unhealthy indwelling develops and how it can even lead to that state the psychiatric profession calls "psychosis."

As a child, a fellow we'll call John not only loves to spend time in his own head, he really isn't very comfortable anywhere else. John has a vivid imagination, dreams up fantasies and stories for himself, draws cartoons of other worlds, and even as a child, he has precious little use for what he already disparagingly calls "the real world." In that real world, mostly hellish things go on, and those things that aren't hellish strike him as intensely boring. Because he experiences the real world as either hellish or boring, he avoids it as best he can.

Can you begin to sense what his mindroom is going to look and feel like? Closed, claustrophobic, dark, impregnable—you can see it, can't you?

John's mother over-praises him, telling him that he is her little genius and that he is destined to change the world. His father belittles him and verbally attacks him. That his mother praises him but does not protect him from his father's verbal abuse is maddening to him. Why not protect him a little more and praise him a little less? Because this makes no sense to him—wouldn't you protect the person destined to change the world, if you really meant what you said? He both despises her and refuses to believe her message that he is super worthy. Her praise contributes to nothing but an inferiority complex.

Can you sense how angry he's becoming in his closed-off mindroom? Maybe even furious?

At the same time, he does feel rather special. He knows that the stories he tells himself are indeed good and lively, that his cartoons are excellent, and that he has some spark or gift different from his boring peers. As a result, he indwells more, relentlessly hiding out and paying less and less attention to the doings at school or in his family. His mindroom may be a dark and angry place, but it is also his castle. And he is a bit of a prince in there, seated on his throne, building resentments and throwing tantrums.

Over time, his sense of agitation and frustration mount. He has no friends, no relaxations, little contact with the world, and nothing to show for all that time spent in isolation. Pestered by all sorts of thoughts, half-dreams, and half-nightmares, his sleeplessness increases. Since his schoolwork bores him silly, he builds up an impressive lack of motivation to do it. As a result, he starts to almost fail at school, pulling off barely passing grades and further flaming his resentments.

Getting a good sense of what it feels like being in John's mindroom, and what it feels like *to be John*?

John starts to build up an impressive lack of coping skills, since he hides out so much and interacts so little with his peers. As smart as he is, he nevertheless finds himself becoming more and more indecisive, since when he's trapped in that claustrophobic mindroom, he can turn any issue over a million different ways and see everything from a million different angles. His grandiosity increases as he fills up notebooks with what he believes to be brilliant cartoons and witty aphorisms, and his sense of inferiority increases as he is snickered at more and more by his peers and belittled more and more by his father. He becomes a god-bug: arrogant and grandiose in his mindroom, and small, unimportant, laughable, and repugnant in the real world.

John is a smart, sensitive, creative boy who is regularly belittled, regularly pressed to succeed, told that he is worthless, and told that he is special. He spends great stretches of time in his room and in his mindroom because the world feels dangerous, because he is awkward around his peers, and because he's gotten into the lifelong habit of staring at his ceiling and obsessively fantasizing. His particular pattern of indwelling becomes habitual, and since it is now habitual, it has that pleasant feel of habit. At the same time, it feels completely unpleasant. How pleasant can it really feel to live in such an airless place, surrounded by grievances and resentments?

Has John already started hearing voices? Maybe. Surely, he is a likely candidate. When and if John does start to hear voices, he is likely to end up in a psychiatrist's office or in the psychiatric ward of a hospital. We know full well what will happen then. Little or nothing about John's actual lived experience or his indwelling style will get investigated, both because John is not up for such investigations and because such investigations are not part of the current "treatment" routine. John will receive a diagnosis of "schizophrenia" or some other "diagnosis" and be put on chemicals called medication.

This is where we must leave John.

Is the picture I'm painting of John indeed what happens in some human beings? Is this one version of unhealthy indwelling? We do not know. But it is surely a reasonable and intuitively sensible possibility. I hope that this hypothetical example helps clarify an idea crucial to our understanding of what "redesigning your mind" really means. We are not just moving furniture around, or installing windows, valves, and exit doors. We are using the power of dynamic self-regulation to upgrade our habitual indwelling style. That's the life-saving, life-enhancing work we've set for ourselves.

· ✦ ○ ✦ ·

Visualization: Visualize your indwelling style. How would you characterize it?

Writing Prompt: Describe what you perceive as the difference between healthy and unhealthy indwelling.

PART III

FURNITURE AND ACCESSORIES

YOUR BEAUTY DRAWER

In Part III, we continue our fanciful but valuable redesign and redecoration process. Remember that each chapter presents a stand-alone idea and a stand-alone visualization: adding just one piece of useful furniture or suggestive accessory will help change how you think and how you experience life.

Next, let's get a nice, sturdy chest of drawers delivered. It can have many, many drawers, a number limited only by the limits of your imagination. To begin, we'll dedicate one drawer to keeping reminders of your essential beauty and talismans that ward off any self-pestering self-criticism. We'll make it your beauty drawer.

In every workshop that I lead, whatever its primary subject, I find it important to remind participants that each of them is the beauty in life. They each have an immaculate center or core that is their essential nature. Our thoughts may be very far from beautiful when we pester ourselves, plot our revenge, complain about life, and in countless other ways darken our own doorstep. Our actions may likewise prove anything but beautiful when we indulge an addiction, fail to show up to our life purposes, and behave far below our standards. But deeply hidden away and difficult to access is that essential loveliness—that humanity, that beauty, that goodness—with which every infant enters the world.

You can better access that splendid core by taking a daily trip to that chest of drawers you've just had delivered and opening the drawer in which you keep your beauty talismans. Remind yourself that you are not your thoughts, not your feelings, not the you who was manic, chaotic, or despairing today, not the you who ate too much at lunch or passed the buck at work. Instead, you're the you who shares genetic wealth with everyone who has ever done the right thing and risen to the occasion.

What will your beauty talismans be? You can have many, given that you have a whole drawer available! One might be a photo of you at the age of four or five—impish, happy, perfect, getting ready to dive into the lake or cut your birthday cake. A second might be a poem you love that captures the poignancy of living, written out in your own hand and decorated like a page out of an illuminated manuscript. A third might be a marble that represents your precious core. What else? You can have so many!

Right now, visualize your own wonderful collection of talismans and mementos that will do an excellent job of reminding you that you are fundamentally precious.

I recently strolled a path surmounting the white chalk cliffs of the English coast. I thought about that D-Day armada that sailed off to liberate Europe. I couldn't help but think that there would be pitched battles and bloodshed until the end of time. The horrors arising out of our human nature may ultimately overwhelm the beauty that is also a feature of that inheritance. In the big picture of armies and tidal waves, what is a marble, a poem, or a photo of you at five? What are they? They are just about everything, really. They inspire you to be your best self and do the next right thing. What else matters more than that?

How might you use your beauty drawer? You might open it every morning as part of your morning routine. You pick out your actual clothes, then visit your mindroom, open your beauty drawer, visit with your talismans, take one or two out to touch and hold, and announce, "I am the beauty in life." Later in the day, maybe when you've done something just a little bit foolish or disappointing, you visit them again and they help you heal. Finally, as part of your bedtime routine, rather than having some anxious thought or some resentment be the last thing on your mind, you visit your beauty drawer and fall asleep gazing at your talismans of worth. Wasn't your day enriched by having spent real time with your richest self?

The theme of this chapter is what is known as disidentification, an idea made popular by Italian psychologist Roberto Assagioli, who developed a branch of psychotherapy known as psychosynthesis. Assagioli explained:

> "We are dominated by everything with which our self is identified. Some people get their identity from their feelings, others from their thoughts, others from their social roles. But this identification with a part of the personality destroys the freedom which comes from the experience of the pure 'I.' "

I am picturing this "pure you" as really beautiful, maybe even as civilization's saving grace. Remember it, keep it alive, and access it by visiting your beauty drawer frequently.

· + ○ + ·

Visualization: Visualize a chest of drawers. Choose one of its drawers as your beauty drawer and fill it with objects that help remind you that you are the beauty in life.

Writing Prompt: What, if anything, is the difference between "you" and your thoughts, feelings, and actions?

YOUR HAT DRAWER

Each of us is a single self, made up of many identities.

You are a person, a Protestant, a watercolor artist, a New Englander, and so forth. The majority of these identities are not consciously adopted or chosen; they are simply who we are and always have been. Other identities we adopt and choose as we live (for example, taking on the identity of a psychoanalyst, expat, or retiree).

The matter of identity is almost as complicated as the matter of mind. For instance, there are at least a score of identities available to any given artist, who may see themselves as more of a beautifier, a trickster, a classicist, and so on. Some of these they wear comfortably; others they may wear rather resentfully. Artists discover over time that they must adopt certain identities whether they want to or not.

Creatives today are obliged to hone marketing, promoting, and entrepreneurial skills that support their creative efforts, and act in public ways that artists of bygone ages did not have to act. Today, a musician is as likely to have a hit because they pull off a stunt as they would be because they pen a brilliant ballad, as likely to be cherished for their celebrity status as for their artistry, and more alert to their media opportunities than to their creative opportunities.

A smart, sensitive, creative person is unlikely to relish these duties and may frankly hate them. This then leads to a roaring internal conflict between what an artist wants to do—make worthy art—and what they are obliged to do—namely, relentlessly market and promote. As it is better for a creative to embrace these tasks and unwanted identity pieces than to wage an inner battle against them, a certain useful inner shift is wanted. Rather than feeling put upon by these duties, accept that many activities in the service of meaning do not themselves feel meaningful. This is a mature attitude worth cultivating, and to help cultivate this positive and adaptive attitude, you might try the following.

Turn to the chest of drawers that you had delivered in the last chapter and designate one of those drawers as your "identity hat drawer." In it are all of the hats that you enjoy wearing, and also all of those hats that you are sometimes obliged to wear. What might that quite crowded hat drawer contain? The hat you wear when you want to be your wildest at the easel. The hat you wear when you want to be your most careful and get all those details right. The hat you wear as you rehearse a meeting with a gallery owner. The hat you wear as you write marketing and promotional copy for your next newsletter. The hat you wear when you switch artist identities for the day and paint as an abstract expressionist rather than as a photorealist. And so on. Let this drawer be phenomenally crowded with hats, so as to provide you with a visual reminder that you have many roles to play in life, many tasks to accomplish, and many identities to juggle.

How will you use this drawer? Say that you've become aware that it is past time to query literary agents about the novel you've just finished writing. You've been able to put off the moment of reckoning by waffling internally about whether you intend to self-publish the novel or try the traditional route. But you've known all along that you meant to try the traditional route and now you can't deny that truth any longer. Still, you're balking—and feeling terrible.

Now that you have your hat drawer available to you, you can try the following. Open your hat drawer. Put on a hat that you enjoy wearing. Maybe it's the hat you associate with writing in the garden or having tea with your sister. Wear that hat for a bit and enjoy the moment. Smile with enjoyment, then sigh and say, "Query email-writing hat, please." Rummage through the drawer and find that hat. Do not disparage it. Do not make faces as you search for it. Do not grumble as you put it on. Give it a good tug to make sure that it's on properly. Then, without angst or drama, work on that query email.

You are obliged to wear many hats in life. Each represents its own set of challenges, like those associated with, say, being a minority member, an immigrant, or a creative in a field where there is little money to be made. The many hats in your hat drawer are there to make you smile and chuckle, but they are also there to remind you just how many tasks come with living authentically.

· + ○ + ·

Visualization: Visualize a hat drawer filled to the brim with hats matching your many identities.

Writing Prompt: Identify your many identities. Let that list be as long as it needs to be. Then, describe the hat that goes with each identify.

YOUR SNOW GLOBE COLLECTION

It's hard to think, calculate, create, meditate, or remember or do much of anything in your mindroom if your mind is too noisy. A noisy mind is the exact equivalent of unnecessary thoughts grabbing hundreds of millions of valuable neurons and stealing them away from the good work they might otherwise be doing. As many billions of neurons as we have, every single unwanted and unnecessary thought grabs a substantial number of them and robs us of our full intellectual powers.

If you are busily thinking that the lawn needs mowing, that you hate your day job, that you've already used up all of your vacation time this year, and that your oven (which needs cleaning) is not self-cleaning, it is highly unlikely that you will also be solving the difficult plot points in your novel. Where will those plot-point solutions come from if billions of your neurons are engaged in all that other thinking?

There are many ways to conceptualize that noise and many ways to reduce it, as some of it needs to be quieted and some of it needs to be addressed but not in a self-pestering, obsessive way. The practices of mindfulness and meditation are popular ways of dealing with those unwanted thoughts. Likewise, you might try a basic anxiety management technique like deep breathing. Framing that noise as a manifestation of anxiety is a solid approach.

Indeed, it may well be the case that the majority of that noise and those neuron-stealing thoughts is the nattering result of ambient anxiety. If it is, then calmness is the answer. Growing calm can produce the quiet you require for good ideas to have the chance to percolate up. You already have a calmness switch to use, which I hope you've been employing. Here's another really useful visualization to try.

Create a lovely snow globe collection and keep it on top of the dresser that you previously had delivered. When you want to quiet your mind and calm yourself, select one of your snow globes, shake it up, and as the snow settles, feel yourself settling, growing calmer and quieter. When life is swirling around you, when your own thoughts are swirling inside of you, and when you can hear nothing but agitated noise in your own mind, select a snow globe and use it to help you settle.

You might employ a single snow globe that you use regularly to calm yourself, or you might enjoy creating a whole snow globe collection and adding to it periodically. When you travel, come upon a Christmas market in an Alpine village, and encounter some charming Bavarian snow globes, add one or two to your mental collection. This activity of collecting snow globes will keep them in mind, remind you of their value, and reinforce the idea that you know how to calm yourself when your mind grows too noisy.

You might adopt this snow globe ceremony as one of the first things you do whenever you enter your mindroom. You've set aside a certain time to write your novel, create your app, or compose your symphony. As agitated as you're feeling, you still manage to send yourself to your mindroom. You switch on the lights using the dual light-and-calmness switch, then head directly to your dresser. You pick a snow globe from your snow globe collection, give it a vigorous shake, and as the snow inside the globe settles, you feel yourself settle. Wouldn't this make for a lovely entrance ritual?

Give it a try right now. Create your first snow globe. What
scene will you choose? A quaint Alpine one? One with
the Eiffel Tower at the center? A cozy Christmas fireplace
scene? One related to the creative work you do: a symphony
orchestra if you're a composer, or a starry night if you're an
astronomer? Create your first snow globe, shake it up, and feel
yourself growing calm and quiet as the snow settles.

If you don't love the first snow globe you create, create
another one. What could be simpler? Create some based on
the books you've written, on elements in the periodic table,
on places to which you've traveled. Try out a huge variety.
There's no cost—and maybe some unlikely one will prove your
calming charm!

· ✦ ○ ✦ ·

Visualization: Visualize using snow globes as
your primary way of calming yourself and quieting
your mindroom.

Writing Prompt: Consider the following question:
"Should I visualize a snow globe collection or should
I buy myself a real snow globe collection?" What
are the pros and cons of a visualization technique
versus a hands-on ceremony?

YOUR MUG COLLECTION

Every morning I take the following pleasure: I open one of my kitchen cupboards and choose my coffee mug for the day. I maintain five or six primary choices and many backup choices. Currently, my six primary mugs represent Paris, London, Prague, New York, Rome, and Berlin. The Paris mug is stenciled with the Paris Metro system. The Prague mug features the famous Charles Bridge. The New York mug features a lot of coffee iconography and reminds me of the cafés I frequented in the West Village as a teenager.

What do these mugs do for me, in addition to holding my coffee? They remind me of my traditions: that humanist values are upheld by the few rather than the many; that great ideas do not come from committees; that, just as I do, other writers have had to sit down and spend a year (or two, or three) getting their words straight in order for fine books to exist; and that a significant handful of folks in every time and place have thumbed their noses at tyrants and ridiculed humbug.

They also remind me of my responsibilities. I am obliged to stand with those freethinkers, humanists, and freedom fighters. Those innocent coffee mugs do a lot for me! You, too, can feel less isolated and alone and can better maintain your motivation by reminding yourself of your traditions. Either employ a mug collection that, for example, celebrates stops on the international bohemian highway, or design some other way of your own choosing. You can maintain them in reality, in your cupboard; or you can maintain them as a visualization, as mugs that exist only in your mindroom.

Which traditions are important to you? Maybe you feel yourself a part of the long tradition of Catholic writers. Maybe you feel more connected to the ancient Greeks, like Plato, Aristotle, Socrates, Democritus, and other natural philosophers of that bygone age, than to any thinkers of today. Maybe something about the lives of expat artists—women painters of the Left Bank, Black musicians of the Paris jazz clubs, Russian ballerinas who danced with Diaghilev and the Ballets Russes—fire your imagination and move your heart. If you feel connected in such ways, create a mug collection to celebrate what you're feeling.

Wake up each morning, visit the room that is your mind, contemplate your mug collection, and select a mug for the day. You may be as alone in your studio or in your lab as a star is in deep space, but you are also connected to all those souls who feel and have felt the same way that you do about jazz, short stories, or abstract math. And remember to regularly add to your collection. There's no cost and you can't possibly run out of room!

A few years ago, I visited Brighton, England, to lead a workshop there. I quickly realized that a Brighton mug had to grace my collection. Brighton struck the right chords and stirred the right emotions. Back in the 1930s, British novelist Graham Greene frequented the pubs dotting the Lanes (the narrow shopping streets near Brighton's seafront) and dreamed up the characters who populated the world of Brighton Rock. You can visit the Greene room upstairs at The Cricketers and peruse the author's framed letters—or, in your mind's eye, you can create a Graham Greene mug for your daily green tea.

In that solitude that every creative person craves and needs, you might begin to feel lonely, isolated, and alienated. Your experience of spending time in the room that is your mind can slip from exquisite to unbearable. If you find yourself thinking, "I am so alone," turn directly to your imagined mug collection. Say, "I am not alone. I am traveling the path so many have traveled before me." Say, "I have many friends on the bohemian highway whom I've never met." Feel comforted by the way that you can embody your cherished traditions and enjoy the past's presence in the room that is your mind.

Of course, a useful coffee mug collection is not a substitute for actual human contact. You will want to supplement celebrating your traditions with actual hugs and kisses, and with the actual tears and bruises that come with intimacy. But needing that vital supplementary reality doesn't change the fact that you are not ever alone, not if you embrace your traditions. You do not need to love or respect those in your lineage—they are just people after all, with their warts and shadows. But they have toiled in the same fields as you toil, and at least with respect to this one love—their love of fiction, their love of freethinking, their love of jazz—they share and have shared your deepest values.

Create your coffee mug collection and celebrate your traditions. If you do, you will feel less alone.

· + ○ + ·

Visualization: Visualize a coffee mug collection. Each morning, select your mug for the day. This ceremony will help connect you with your intellectual and creative traditions.

Writing Prompt: Play with the phrase "international bohemian highway." Does that phrase hold some resonance for you?

YOUR LIFE-PURPOSE CHINA

It is painfully easy for a contemporary, post-modern person to begin to doubt that they or any of their efforts really matter. Why spend so much time, sweat, and blood crafting a poem? Why throw all of your intellectual eggs into the basket of string theory when string theory may prove a passing fancy? Why turn your whole life over to literary criticism when the books you are teaching now bore you? Why provide another mental disorder diagnosis to another client when you've stopped believing in the logic or legitimacy of diagnosing? Why bother with any of this?

This common problem—a sense of lost purpose and the experience of encroaching meaninglessness—is best counteracted in the following way. You remind yourself (or perhaps explain to yourself for the first time) that you do not intend to make the mistake of believing that there is a single "meaning" or "purpose" to life. Rather, you are going to get behind the idea that there are multiple life-purpose choices that you can and must make, and that you can do a beautiful job of identifying and embracing another one of your life-purpose choices when a current choice happens to feel stale and empty.

If today, writing poetry does not feel especially meaningful to you, you can decide to embrace your life-purpose choice of relationships and go to the zoo with your daughter. Or maybe you'll decide to embrace your life-purpose choice of service and volunteer your time at a homeless shelter. Or maybe you'll decide to embrace your life-purpose choice of activism and engage in some real work in support of a cause that matters to you. Or maybe you'll decide to embrace some other life-purpose choice that feels alive and available. Then tomorrow, you can see if returning to your poetry, your string theory, your literary criticism, or your clinical practice feels less dull and beside the point. It indeed might, by virtue of you having taken a vacation from it and having spent some time engaged in another meaningful pursuit.

You can help remind yourself of how to keep meaning afloat by visualizing a set of life-purpose china that you store in the room that is your mind and use for existential snacking. Take a moment right now and think through what dozen motifs you want displayed on your dinner service—that is, take a moment and create your menu of life purposes. On that list might be important "doing" activities, like creating, relating, serving, and truth-telling, and equally important "ways of being" states, like being calm, passionate, or authentic. Your life-purpose choices might include "my health," "speaking up for children," "supporting my mate's career," or "moving evolutionary theory forward." Create your menu now.

Say that writing poetry has started to feel pointless. Go to your mindroom, head to the cupboard you've installed, and pull out your full set of life-purpose china—the eight, ten, or twelve life-purpose dinner plates that make the complete service.

Next lay out the plates, each hand-painted with one of your life-purpose choices. Choose one plate for your upcoming snack. Maybe you'll choose your activism plate. Maybe you'll choose your mystery-writing plate. Maybe you'll choose your career plate. Maybe you'll choose your friendship plate. Maybe you'll choose your "being calm" plate. Maybe you'll choose your "being passionate" plate. Pick a plate, get out some silverware, and prepare your "meaning-making" snack.

Bring out your scones, butter, and jams. Fix yourself a lovely snack on the life-purpose plate you've chosen. As you munch, daydream about how you intend to live that particular life purpose today. Will you take your daughter to the zoo? Ah, maybe it's too chilly for that. Then might you take her to visit an art museum? That might be fun! You could teach her all about drawing outside the lines and speaking in her own voice. That would make for a lovely few hours! Finish your snack and go do exactly that. Take her on that excellent field trip.

It is easy to forget—or to never have learned—that you have many life-purpose choices available to you. Your set of life-purpose china, each plate decorated with a different life-purpose choice, can provide you with an important reminder of that score and help keep you existentially healthy. And if you happen to break one of your imaginary plates, it will prove a snap to replace!

· ✢ ○ ✢ ·

Visualization: Visualize a set of life-purpose china that you employ to remind yourself that you have many life-purpose choices available to you, if and when you decide to name those choices, honor them, and live them.

Writing Prompt: If you haven't done so already, play with the idea of creating your list or menu of life-purpose choices.

YOUR OTHER SHOE RACK

Here's another use for the closet you installed in your mindroom, where you already store your straitjacket and hang up your heavy winter overcoat. It is also the place where you keep a shoe rack filled not with your shoes, but with the shoes of others. These many pairs of shoes help you empathize with the folks you're obliged to interact with—if you're a writer, folks like your editor, literary agent, or publicist.

Empathy is a word that developmental psychologists use. If our parents were genuinely responsive to our needs, it is likely that we developed an ability to empathize with others. But millions of people, perhaps even the majority, had a poorer experience that resulted in lifelong relational difficulties. Be that as it may, it is the job of each of us to heal those wounds (if we were wounded in that way) and make the conscious decision to treat the people around us decently.

Empathy is the ability and the willingness to understand another person's thoughts and feelings. It is the mind-reading, feeling-reading ability built into each of us that many people have trouble accessing and often do not want to access. It's in many ways an inconvenient ability, because it can make the people around us suddenly real—and how much more convenient it would be if they remained unreal! If they did, we could treat them as props, puppets, servants, inconveniences, or furniture.

Why is it important to empathize? Say that you're a creative person who wants a career in one of the art disciplines. If you don't really "get" what marketplace players are thinking and feeling, you are much less likely to be able to deal with them or sell to them. The better you understand other people, the better your chances are for success.

Take the following example. You sell a book to an editor. The book comes out. You present them with an idea for a second book and they decline. If you take their "no" at face value and don't take an interest in what they are thinking and feeling or what is going on in their world, all you are left with is that "no." If instead you empathize with them as a person and with their position as editor, at the very least you've created the chance to obtain more information.

Empathizing in this instance means understanding your editor's reality. This has two separate meanings: understanding them as a person and understanding their role in their publishing house. Are they, as a *person*, someone who makes snap decisions, but who can be invited to rethink that snap decision based on rational arguments? Are they, as an *editor*, someone who has to answer to a lot of people about their decisions and who therefore needs to be armed—by you— with lots of ammunition to present to those other people? If you don't know these things, then you won't know how much ammunition to present them with when you propose a project, or how to help them change their mind after they've said "no" to a project.

In this particular usage of the word "empathy," its antonym is not "unfeelingness" but "misunderstanding." The proof that we are not empathizing with people is that we find ourselves not understanding where they're coming from. If you send your editor an email and you somehow take it personally that they haven't replied to you in twenty-four hours, you are almost surely misunderstanding where they are coming from

in not answering quickly. If you have given them something
that they actually have to think about, it should follow that
they need some time to think about it!

Most creatives are susceptible to these misunderstandings for
two primary reasons. The first is that they don't get sufficient
opportunity to deal with marketplace players, and as a result,
they don't have a clear picture of who they are, how they
operate, and what their universe looks like. The second is that
because marketplace players matter so much to them and
make them so anxious, they can't think very clearly about who
these people really are. What can help? The following.

When you're obliged to deal with a marketplace player, go
to your mindroom, proceed to your closet, and put on a pair
of that person's shoes. Marketplace players are lionized,
demonized, fantasized about, and so on—but rarely are they
thought about clearly. By putting on that person's shoes and
feeling how they pinch, you give yourself the opportunity to
think as clearly about them as you can.

· + ○ + ·

> **Visualization:** Visualize a shoe rack where you
> store pairs of shoes that belong to the people
> you know, the people you are obliged to interact
> with, and the people you love. When you want to
> understand one of these folks, put on a pair of their
> shoes and experience what it's like to walk a mile in
> their shoes.
>
> **Writing Prompt:** How interested are you in
> understanding other people? A lot? A little? Not
> much at all?

YOUR POWER BAR DRAWER

Many competent people do not have their demonstrable competence translate into self-confidence. They squirm and wriggle in the room that is their mind and say things like "I can't do this," "I'm not equal to that," and "I had surely better not try that other thing!"

As a result, they live a reduced life and may even forfeit their dreams. They do not write their novel, start their business, or push physics forward. They get many things done quite nicely, but not the most important ones. How terrible! Let's create a visualization for that.

Let's stock our mindroom with a plentiful supply of power bars that provide tons of energy and lots of instantly renewed confidence. Add those power bars to your mental arsenal! Line a drawer in your dresser with some prettily patterned shelf paper and stock it with all sorts of power bars. You get to pick your flavors. How about peanut butter chocolate? Oatmeal raisin walnut? Hard and crunchy? Soft and chewy? All up to you!

You also get to design the wrappers and name your brand of confidence. What will you call these power bars? Maybe "Super confidence boost!" or "I can absolutely do this!"? Design the logo, pick your colors, select your graphics, and create an array of confidence boosters that are not just tasty, they're also beautiful, like a gorgeous label on a wine bottle or an exquisite box from an upscale chocolatier. Go ahead and create your product line and stock your pantry right now!

How might you use these power bars? Say that you have a long-standing dream to build an online business that works so well and produces so much income that you can travel anywhere you like and hop around the world. You're aware that some people are doing this, you know that you're pretty skillful, savvy, and resourceful, and the only thing standing in the way is...what exactly? What has kept you from pursuing this dream of yours?

Well, many things. Maybe you don't actually have a solid idea for your business. And there are so many come-ons with hefty price tags guaranteeing that with no effort you can make millions online—those come-ons turn you off. Plus, a paycheck is a paycheck. Plus, you don't have the time, the energy, the tech skills, or the connections! So instead of pursuing your dream, you throw in the towel for another day, another week, another month, and another year.

You're very aware that it all comes down to a failure of nerve and a shortfall of confidence.

Use your confidence power bars! Don't give up on your dream just because your confidence is failing you. Don't throw up your hands and dismiss your idea as ridiculous or beyond reach. Instead, grab a confidence power bar. Go to the room that is your mind, open the drawer where you keep your power bars, take a moment to survey your array—the champagne and dark chocolate ones, the salted caramel ones, the blueberry and granola ones—and choose your power boost.

Unwrap it slowly. Take a bite. Savor the taste. Feel your confidence returning. Feel the boost. Use that burst of energy to propel you to do something in the service of your dream. Maybe that something is just walking, breathing, and thinking. Maybe that something is making a list. Maybe that something is finding free internet information from generous dreamers who have made their personal business dreams work. And if your confidence slips, have another bar! They contain no calories. You can nibble on them as often as you like without gaining an ounce!

The mind is the place where we lose our confidence. Our knees may buckle and our throat may tighten, but that's because our mind weakened those body parts. The mind is also the place where we can regain confidence. We can say things to ourselves that serve and support us. We can say, "I have an excellent novel in me and I'm going to write it," or "I'm going to make that online business work and finally move away from here!" If you feel your confidence waning, you know what to do: go directly to that drawer marked "Eat me!" and grab a bite of confidence.

· ✚ ○ ✚ ·

Visualization: Visualize a drawer full of confidence-boosting power bars.

Writing Prompt: Name and describe a project that you would tackle if you had more confidence.

YOUR SELECTION TABLE

The people I coach have many projects in mind and many projects in progress. You may be in this same position of having to juggle multiple worthwhile and important projects.

For example, an independent filmmaker might be in post-production on one film, raising money on a second film, entering a third completed film into film festivals, and contemplating several next films. A neuroscientist might be working on a popular book about the mind, a textbook about his specialty, several journal articles, and some new experiments meant to buttress his hypotheses. Often enough, this is too much to handle, resulting in one or another of the following unfortunate outcomes.

Having so many choices can easily cause a creative to throw up their hands, announce that it's all too much, and do nothing in support of their creative efforts. Months may pass this way, even years. Every day they know that they ought to be doing something, anything, and every day they make themselves sad and disappointed by not choosing and acting. That jumble and welter of choices remains so daunting that, despite how they feel not doing anything, they continue to avoid their work.

Or, so as to reduce their anxiety about choosing, they may choose one of their projects and work on it obsessively, to the point of excluding all their other projects. They may do this even though they know for certain that they really ought to be submitting their completed film to film festivals and tackling all of the post-production details on their other film, and not focusing so completely on this fledgling film. But this fledgling film fascinates them, and they try to justify their obsession by arguing, for example, that their mind can only successfully tackle one thing at once. At the same time, they know that they're treating their finished film and their almost-finished film unfairly.

Having too many choices results in other negative outcomes as well. Unable to choose among the many articles they might write, a would-be professor may never acquire the tenure they so desperately want. Unable to choose among which of their images to market, a would-be graphic designer may find themselves spending all their time at the service of their paying clients and none of their time building their own business. The list of negative outcomes from a painful multiplicity of choices is very long. What is a creative to do?

One thing to try is adding a selection table to your mindroom. This table might look like a drafting table, a cleared-off desk, an antique card table, or any sort of table large enough to hold the choices in question. When you're burdened by all these choices and you feel ready to throw up your hands and choose nothing, say to yourself, "Selection table time." Stride directly to your selection table, lay out your choices, and choose.

Our filmmaker would lay out their completed film, their almost-completed film, their fledgling film, and their ideas for future films and say, "All right, what's next?" or "All right, what shall I choose for this evening?" or some other phrase meant to signify that they're not choosing for all time, they're choosing just for today, just for the next hour, even just for the next twenty minutes. They make their choice and then act.

Maybe they go online and submit the finished film to a film festival, however tedious that process may be. Maybe they get in touch with the composer who is supposed to score their almost-finished film and try to get clarity on when the score will be done, however difficult writing that email may feel. Maybe they give themselves the treat of working a bit on a new idea. Because of this new commitment to careful choosing, they don't have to worry that working on this new idea will derail them or begin to consume them.

Use this selection table to enter into a new, less anxious, more powerful relationship to choosing. This selection table can become one of the more important items of furniture in your mindroom. Maybe, before you go to it, you use one of your snow globes to calm yourself or warm your hands by the fire you've built, so as to feel your passion rekindled. Maybe you create a ritual or ceremony that you repeat whenever you have to choose: blazing fire, snow globe, selection table. By getting into this great habit, you stop being daunted by choosing.

If you have some choice to make that you know needs your attention, use your new selection table to make that choice right now.

· ✦ ○ ✦ ·

Visualization: Visualize a selection table that you use to lay out and make your choices.

Writing Prompt: When you have many potential projects that you might work on, what tends to happen?

YOUR AWARENESS SCREEN

I'd like you to install a good-sized television screen opposite your comfy easy chair. Use that screen to view how you currently operate and how you might improve your operations.

Consider the following common problem facing writers, painters, composers, and other creatives. Creative folks often leave their creative work too soon, putting in twenty minutes or half an hour and then getting anxious, confused, or defeated and abandoning their work. Maybe they get derailed by a stray thought like "I have no idea what I'm doing!" Maybe some fear—that what they're creating isn't very good, that it won't be liked, or that it will never sell—frightens them out of the studio. Maybe some distraction from the outside world—a truck rumbling by—breaks their working trance, leaving them suddenly resistant to resuming. Whatever the reason, the spell is broken and the work ends.

Imagine that this is your problem. And imagine that, seated in your easy chair in front of a blazing fire, you could watch these antics of yours played out on the screen above the mantel. You'd shake your head in dismay and exclaim, "Wow, did I really leave that easily? I won't do that again!" Maybe some simple, brilliant solution will occur to you, for instance, "Gee, what if I just got up and stretched rather than outright running away? Maybe after just a little stretching and breathing, I'd be able to get right back to work!"

The beauty of all this occurring in the room that is your mind is that you can use the screen above your mantel to not only watch your antics, but also to view any changes you decide to make and whatever transformations occur. Now, sitting there, instead of seeing yourself flee the studio at the first disruptive thought, you see yourself calmly rise, stretch a bit, stroll about a bit, and—maybe even with a smile on your face—resume your creative efforts. Wasn't that lovely to watch? And didn't that seem completely plausible?

Let's take another example. Say that you want to radically change how you use your lunch break at your day job. First, you'd watch how lunch currently goes. There you are, checking your emails for the millionth time, doing this and that on your phone. Now, run the reel of the lunch hour that you want. There you are, standing up, striding out of the office, and making straight for the park two blocks down. The sun is shining. You sketch for twenty minutes, savor your sushi lunch (extra pickled ginger, light on the wasabi), and then stroll back, entranced by the light. Isn't it easier to pick the lunch that you want when you can see it up there on that screen?

You can watch a whole day in a matter of seconds. Say that you decide you would like to exhaust yourself in the service of your creative work every Saturday. You intend to work from five o'clock in the morning until two in the afternoon on your current suite of paintings. Using your screen, you can view how such a day might play itself out. Maybe you notice that by eight o'clock, you're already half-exhausted. What to do? Maybe that's the perfect time for a breakfast break. So you play that out on your big screen and watch yourself take a breakfast break at eight.

Ah, but you see yourself lingering at the kitchen table, spending too much time surfing the internet on your phone.

Well, just change that. Have yourself hop right up after that second cup of coffee rather than procrastinate with a third cup. Okay! You are back to work. What do you see next? Maybe the next challenge comes at about eleven o'clock, when some dreadful fatigue overtakes you. What to do? Ah, a hot shower seems right! You take your shower and get back to work. Now one o'clock is approaching and you're not sure you can get another stitch done. Well then, maybe one o'clock is the real outer limit, not two. If it is, clean up and celebrate!

Use this screen to play out both what is and what ought to be. See how you currently interact with gallery owners, and how you would like to interact instead. Watch yourself avoid completing a painting, and watch yourself complete it. Watch yourself giving an interview, and watch yourself giving a better one. You can use your mindroom awareness screen to reality-test and create an upgraded version of yourself—one that, when you see it up there on the screen, makes you smile and applaud.

· + ○ + ·

Visualization: Visualize a large screen on the wall opposite your easy chair that you use to view how you operate in life and how you would prefer to operate in life.

Writing Prompt: Imagine that you're a documentary filmmaker making a film of your future. What would you like that film to look like?

YOUR REHEARSAL MIRROR

Let's alternate that screen that you just installed with a mirror. You'll use this mirror to watch yourself speak. This may prove to be among the hardest things that you will yourself to do in your mindroom, but it's an extremely important effort to make.

Most folks find it difficult to describe what they do to others or powerfully advocate for that work. This is true for coaches, painters, yoga teachers, and all of the other millions of self-employed solopreneurs. This difficulty lessens their chances of interesting the marketplace in their wares, whether those wares are coaching sessions, landscapes, or yoga classes.

Preparing your pitches in front of the mirror you install in your mindroom can help reduce your fear, your social anxiety, and your performance anxiety. It can also help you dramatically increase your skill level as a confident advocate for your work.

How might you use this mirror? Say that you're an art photographer with a penchant for creating macabre photographs. For your last series, you photographed roadkill that you transported to mountain clearings. The images are striking, but they're also off-putting and hard sell. Your photographs may be wonderful, but few people are interested in buying them. It is your job, and no one else's, to create language that helps you sell them. You can accomplish the task of creating this language with the help of your mirror.

Rather than complaining, "Those Philistines know nothing about art!" or stubbornly repeating, "My photos speak for themselves!" visit the room that is your mind. Begin by using your snow globe collection to calm yourself, or your mug collection to be reminded of your traditions, and then murmur, "How can I use language to support these excellent photos?"

Maybe a phrase will suddenly come to you: "There are no accidents in wild places." How interesting. Might that work? You look in the mirror and repeat, "There are no accidents in wild places." You discover that you not only love that phrase, but just like that, the photo series has acquired additional meaning for you. You now have some powerful language to exploit—and new marketing motivation as well.

We feel more powerful and more self-confident when we train ourselves to speak in short, crisp sentences with real periods at the end of them. If our communication style is to produce long, tortured sentences full of apologies, disclaimers, and other weaknesses, it is vital that we learn to change that style and opt for brevity and power. In front of your mindroom mirror, practice those crisp bits of language.

For example, in anticipation of meeting with a gallery owner, you might practice saying, "I have a large network of loyal admirers." In anticipation of a conversation with a friend who is asking for too much of your time, you might practice saying, "I have to paint today." In anticipation of a conversation with your mate about your right to keep creating even though your efforts aren't bringing in much money, you might practice saying, "I will make money this year." If your mate rolls their eyes and replies, "Oh, really? How?" you might reply in your newly practiced way, "By working really hard and by proving the exception."

Likewise, you can use your mirror to practice telling yourself the truth. It can be the place where you let down your guard, look yourself in the eye, and say, "I am really sad." Maybe it's been hard to make that admission. To make it is to bring up all those areas of your life that may not be working very well, from your tiresome day job to your lack of success as a creative, to your chronic problems with life purpose and meaning. Here, in front of your mindroom mirror, you bravely make that admission, sigh, and wonder, "Mirror, mirror on the wall, what should I do?" Maybe you'll receive back a little magical advice from your wisest self.

Add a mirror to your mindroom and learn to bravely face it. Our natural defenses and our everyday resistance to practicing new habits may make this difficult, but the results—among them better advocacy for your creative efforts, increased self-confidence, and a more powerful communication style—are worth the effort.

· + ○ + ·

Visualization: Visualize a mirror that you use to practice and rehearse crisp speaking, powerful advocacy, and brave truth-telling.

Writing Prompt: What "speeches" ought you be rehearsing more?

YOUR CRYSTAL BALL

You may not do something very well right now. That doesn't mean that you won't do that same thing beautifully down the road. Because this is true, you will want to include a crystal ball among your mindroom's furnishings and decorations, one that you'll use to predict improvement and success. That's a really useful addition!

What sorts of improvements and successes? Here's what I have in mind. One winter evening, I find myself in the green room of a beautiful new theater on campus at University of North Carolina School of the Arts, waiting to give a creativity chat to a crowd of several hundred North Carolinians. I'd given this chat many times before, varying the title to suit the audience but presenting essentially the same material. I can now deliver it on a dime, starting up the instant you say "Go!" and ending directly on the hour. In fact, when I delivered this chat to a group of Indiana arts administrators, what impressed the conference chair the most (more than the chat's content) was the fact that I ended so promptly!

Nowadays, I deliver my chat without any notes (although I keep a sheet handy with some headlines in case I blank out). This is a far cry from my early days of speaking in support of my books. In 1992, I gave my first book talk at Green Apple Books, an independent bookstore in the Richmond District of San Francisco, located on a street of Chinese vegetable markets and Russian bakeries. I had no clue what I was doing.

It wasn't that I hadn't prepared—no, indeed—but *what* I'd prepared was wondrously odd and constituted the strangest chat that any audience had ever had to suffer through.

Instead of describing *Staying Sane in the Arts* (the book I was promoting), or simpler yet, reading from it (as most writers on tour do), I prepared a cross between a stump speech and an academic white paper on something I called "The Artist Corps." I think I meant the speech to be a visionary call to arms on the order of "I have a dream…for artists." It might have fit the bill if I'd been delivering it on the Washington Mall to a crowd of a million marching artists. To this small crowd, drifting in off Clement Street after shopping for sugar snap peas and piroshki, it was a bore and a monstrosity. To further make them wish that they had chosen the comedy club across the street, I read the darned thing, slowly (to give it weight) and softly (because I speak softly). Slowly but surely, everyone walked out.

Eventually I wandered home, dazed but not at all crestfallen. What went through my mind was the following question: "I wonder what would work better?" It took me a while—some years—to figure that "better" out, but I did know to retire that Artists Corps speech and never dust it off again. And, in fact, I got much better!

There was a six-month period during the early '60s when Bob Dylan progressed so fast that he was unrecognizable from the beginning to the end of the year. By December, his playing, his songs, and even his voice (which you wouldn't think could improve dramatically) were a quantum leap better. He wasn't Bob Dylan in January. He was only Bob Dylan in December.

I, too, improved. The journey from the Green Apple chat to the UNC School of the Arts chat was more than a dozen years and three thousand miles. It was that nonlinear distance known as a learning curve. I'd learned how to speak in public. This is very important news. You, too, can expect to improve, and that crystal ball you keep in your mindroom can help you see that much improved, much more successful future.

If you were there at Green Apple Books that evening in 1992, I pity you. I know you'd never have guessed that the stiff, boring fellow reading his speech would one day approach oratory. Fooled you! You, too, may appear one year in support of your first book and make a hash of your presentations and your interviews; and then two years later, having learned a ton, you may appear in support of your second book and sound like Kennedy in Berlin. The task is not to get it right the first time. The tasks are to learn from your pratfalls, and by learning, improve. Your crystal ball can help remind you that this is entirely possible.

And so, where will you put it? Look around your mindroom. Give your crystal ball a place of honor.

· ✦ ○ ✦ ·

Visualization: Visualize a crystal ball that you use to see into a future of improvements and successes.

Writing Prompt: Write on the question, "Do I or don't I believe that I can get better at things?"

YOUR HOPE CHEST

When the great French novelist and existential writer Albert
Camus painted a smile of victory on the face of his famous
character Sisyphus, he was not being true to life. Sisyphus had
been condemned by the gods to roll stones up a mountain
for all eternity, but he nevertheless smiled at his predicament
because he could still thumb his nose at his fate. In real life,
human beings rarely smile when hope is stolen from them.

Human beings rarely smile in prisons, in prisoner-of-war
camps, or in refugee camps. They rarely smile when they lose
their children. They rarely smile when the work they do—or
even the very prospect of work—stops interesting them and
they hold no hope of ever using themselves productively.
They rarely smile when their body stops working well. They
rarely smile when they give up hope of being treated fairly,
of rising out of poverty, of making themselves proud by their
efforts. In these and many other circumstances, loss of hope is
what happens most often.

What does it take to retain hope when having hope makes
little sense? Few answers have worked as well as religion,
where you are offered a better life elsewhere to make up for
the difficulties in this one. In that better life, you will meet
your slain children, the ones you can't stop mourning. In that
better life, you will finally be free of pain and have everything
you ever dreamed of wanting. In that better life, you can stop
toiling mindlessly and finally escape oppression. Religion
provides a satisfying reason for smiling now: a wonderful
eternity to come.

However, if you believe that there are no gods, there is no heaven, and nothing better is coming to mitigate this life, religion won't work for you. How can hope make sense then? Aren't you more inclined to drink yourself into oblivion, sleepwalk through the motions of life, or keep feverishly busy with one pointless enthusiasm after another rather than muster hope? Hope for what, after all?

This lack of hope can ruin our mental health. Existential thinkers have characteristically provided two related answers: rebelliously thumb your nose at the facts of existence and hope anyway, even though hope is absurd. These answers satisfy us in the corner of our being that appreciates irony and rebellion. But they do not work quite well enough in the face of real feelings of hopelessness. There isn't quite enough meat on those bones.

It is hard to get out of bed just to thumb your nose and smile ironically at a universe that doesn't care one way or the other whether you've decided to get out of bed. Maybe that can prove motivation for one day out of seven, but what about the other six? If your mental health requires that you maintain hope, but you find yourself no longer believing that hope makes any sense, what can you do?

One thing you can try is creating a hope chest that you keep in the room that is your mind. This hope chest amounts to yet another effort—maybe a last-ditch effort—to keep hope afloat. It is the place you go to ask the question, "What in here can I still hope for?" You rummage inside and cross your fingers that you will land on something worth the candle. You might discover that:

- You can still hope to love.
- You can still hope for the small enjoyments that you have always enjoyed.

- You can still hope to stand up for your principles and make a tiny difference in the world.

- You can still hope to fight the enemies of reason.

- You can still hope to wrestle something beautiful into existence.

- You can still hope that your efforts will bring a few people some small comfort.

Ask yourself the question, "Have I lost hope?" and honestly answer it. If you discover that you have lost hope, go directly to the room that is your mind, create a hope chest, and fill it with talismans of hope. What will you include? Photographs? Quotations? Memories? Prophecies? Bark from a cherry tree? A miniature particle accelerator? Your choices can be gigantic, tiny, ephemeral, solid—anything you need them to be. This is your hope chest to fill as you require.

Be with these talismans. Losing hope happens. If you've lost hope, you have the job of restoring it. Make an effort to restore it by filling a hope chest and by visiting that chest whenever hope disappears or threatens to evaporate.

· ✦ ○ ✦ ·

Visualization: Visualize a hope chest that you use to keep hope afloat.

Writing Prompt: What can you still hope for? Do some writing on that question.

DESPAIRING MARY

Let's spend a moment or two considering some of the special challenges that come with the creative life.

If you're built with a desire to innovate, won't you feel sad if you don't meet your own expectations, or you don't manage to accomplish much that is innovative? If you're built to fall in love with words, images, music, or movement, and at the same time built with the urge to express yourself and make meaning through creating, won't you feel sad if you don't get the chance to create or perform?

Likewise, if you understand the difference in value between saving a life and taking a photograph, and if you much prefer photography to medicine, won't you feel something like sadness about your own "selfish" choice? And what if you actually master your instrument? What if you play the violin like a master, but there are only a handful of jobs in the whole world equal to your aspirations? Won't you feel sad if you don't land one of those terribly scarce jobs?

We could go on. The headline is that if you are built to walk the path of a creative person, you will find yourself confronted by many special challenges. Such was the case with Mary. In the days when I worked as a psychotherapist, I saw a woman named Mary who was struggling with many challenges—especially with sadness. She framed the matter in the following way:

> "I find everything depressing. I want to love my husband, but I really prefer my solitude. When I do

manage to carve out time to write, I hate working on my novel. Plus, the state of the publishing industry is so depressing. One in a thousand writers, or maybe one in a million writers, make enough money to live. Plus, I find myself eating all the time—mostly junk food. And I hate where we live, in the middle of middle America among people I don't respect. The whole thing is so depressing!"

Mary, by virtue of her creative nature, was likely born with a readiness to become sad, and her life experiences were indeed making her sad. Of course, she couldn't help but use the word "depression" in describing her situation, as nowadays we are all trained to think that way and to speak that way. But as we discussed natural sadness versus "clinical depression," Mary began to reframe matters in terms of personal responsibility rather than in terms of the medical model. She wondered if she could "release her sadness" as she came to describe her newly formed intention.

The image that came to her was of an open window and the sadness wafting away. She pictured one of her mind windows opening onto the sea. She began the practice of entering her mindroom, taking off her heavy overcoat, sitting for a moment in her easy chair, and then proceeding to the window. The window would open effortlessly at her touch. She'd feel the sea breeze on her face, smell the ocean, and consciously let her sadness escape. Her sadness would leave as ghostly streamers that disappeared in the far distance, where the sea met the horizon.

I'd like you to think about personalizing your experience in your mindroom by adopting a sequence that actively changes your indwelling style and helps you deal with some issue like sadness. Consider glancing back over the table of contents

to remind yourself of the many visualizations available
to you, and then create a sequence of perhaps four, five, or
six actions designed to address some challenge. See if you
might be willing to do that. Such a sequence might serve
you beautifully.

· + O + ·

Visualization: Identify an issue that you're
wrestling with and visualize a mindroom sequence
designed to address that issue.

Writing Prompt: Has your experience of inhabiting
your mindroom changed as you've proceeded
through this book?

INCOMPLETE ADAM

One spring, I found myself in London presenting at the First World Congress for Existential Therapy. On a free afternoon, I met with a new client at The Freemasons Arms, a pub just off Hampstead Heath. My new client was a tall, thin University of London professor of history by the name of Adam who, as he told me in an introductory email, had never finished writing a single book he'd begun.

We sat in the back garden with our pints. It was a glorious spring day and the garden was full.

"I write drafts," Adam said.

"Drafts are good," I replied, smiling.

"If they lead to finished books. For me, they don't."

I waited.

"Let me tell you a little bit about myself," he commenced. "I grew up with mentally ill parents. After years of therapy, I think I've come to identify a kind of demon who comes into my consciousness and does not want me to be productive or successful. That demon was born in childhood. It somehow has to do with safety. It did not feel safe living with my parents, plus they *told us* that the world wasn't a safe place. They filled our lives with continual anxiety and catastrophizing."

I nodded and waited.

"Here's how that all plays out. My creativity starts to flow and then anxiety floods in. I tear up the work, I tear myself down, and I abandon the project as no good. I'm also flooded with feelings of intense dread all the time, especially at night. During the day, I always find ways to avoid entering my writing space." He takes a sip. "That's easy enough, as I have classes to teach, committee meetings, a bit of a commute, and all the rest. It's supremely easy to avoid my study. I can't tell you what a shame that is, since my study is so lovely." He laughed briefly. "I wanted to say, 'lovely and inviting,' but it doesn't invite me."

"You've started many books?"

"Many."

"All on sort of the same subject?"

"Yes. The year 1946 as it played out in England, France, and Germany. Something about that postwar year has always intrigued me. But the landscape is vast—larger than vast. One small event in any one of those countries could be worth a book. I get overwhelmed."

"Yes." I nodded. "So the whole tableau feels impossible to capture? But any piece of it feels too small to bother with?"

"That's accurate. Plus, my peers keep writing about that time period, as it seems to have gotten under the skin of countless European historians—rather like your Civil War still hypnotizes so many of your historians. And so every time I hear one of my peers talk about their latest book or article, or watch them perform beautifully at a conference where they share their ideas, that further contributes to my inner difficulties. Those experiences just map onto an already existing damaged force field within some dark, trance-like inner blackness or darkness."

We sat quietly.

"These demons have made it harder for me to keep meaning afloat in my life. They've made it harder for me to keep despair at bay. They've made it harder for me to live my life purposes, and they've contributed to my anxiety and depression diagnoses. It's all of a piece. I've come a certain distance in all this and I can function, but I'm still searching for answers. I'm still wanting to finish some damned book. So here I am."

We were getting near to needing another pint.

"I think that the bottom line for me is that the demon just won't budge, because it is about core safety," Adam said quietly. "Therefore, I probably must celebrate lesser forms of creativity where the emotional stakes and pressures are low. An article, maybe, though articles aren't easy either! I haven't found ways to conquer the demons of darkness, but I do intend to continue to work on this block through some kind of inner-demon work. I haven't quite given up. Not quite."

"What project would you like to get completed?" I wondered aloud.

He shook his head. "I can't get close to thinking about that."

"Talking about it now makes you anxious?"

"Completely!"

"Okay. Let's try the following. I'd like you to picture a snow globe. You know what I mean?"

"Yes. Bizarrely enough, I collect them."

"Great! Let's put a scene in the one we're picturing. How about the South Bank and the London Eye?"

"All right," he consented. "Should I include the Tate Modern? And all the bridges? And the motor launches heading toward Greenwich?"

I had to laugh. This is exactly how anxiety manifests. This manifestation is sometimes incorrectly called "perfectionism"—in Adam's case, the need to create the perfect scene in his imagined snow globe. But "getting it perfect" has nothing to do with it.

"Not to worry," I laughed. "Just shut your eyes now. Picture that snow globe. Now shake it up. A great snowstorm has hit London," I said, smiling. "Got that picture?"

"I do." He shook his head. "A fairly rare occurrence."

"But not in snow globes."

"Indeed."

We both smiled.

"Now, calmly watch the snow settle," I continued. "That great storm is getting lighter and lighter. It's hardly a flurry now. As the snow settles, let your nerves settle. When the snow has settled, let's try my question again."

He sat with his eyes shut. After a few more moments he nodded, eyes still closed.

"All right," I said. "What book would you like to get written?"

He sighed heavily. "One about how Nazi collaborators were treated in those three countries in that first postwar year."

"That's still a lot," I said.

"But perhaps...manageable."

Adam and I worked together for the next three years, chatting via Zoom once a month. There were many downs, but there were also enough ups that Adam finished a draft of his book, dealt with its several revisions, sent it on its journey into the world of academic presses, tolerated the criticisms and rejections it initially received, enjoyed the moment that it was accepted for publication, suffered when its editor made countless demands before seeing it as suitable for publication, and so on. I kept reminding him, "This is the process." At some point, he began to beat me to the punch and became the first to announce, "I know, this is the process!"

The book actually made a small splash, which few books put out by academic presses do. This doesn't quite make Adam happy, as happiness is an elusive commodity in the lives of sentient beings. But it does make Adam smile. Yes, that smile may have been tinged with a good bit of irony, but it is nevertheless warming on those gloomy London days that are bound to come around again.

· ✛ ○ ✛ ·

Visualization: You've encountered more than forty visualizations so far. Pick one and practice it.

Writing Prompt: Do you dream about tackling some large project, but thinking about it makes you too anxious to begin? Write on the question, "How can I get my dream project off the ground?"

OUR THREE PERSONALITIES

We've been employing some useful constructs and metaphors, among them the physical space we're calling your mindroom, your way of being in that physical space we're calling indwelling, and the activity of rethinking that space and rethinking your indwelling style that we're calling redesigning your mind. Let's add another useful construct and metaphor, that your personality is made up of three constituent parts: your original personality, your formed personality, and your available personality.

Our original personality includes everything with which we come into the world: our particular biology, our particular heredity, our particular consciousness, our particular temperament, our particular nervous system, our particular intelligence, our particular sensing apparatus, our particular orientations, our particular readinesses.

Our formed personality is how our original personality, exposed to life experience, begins to solidify into the stiff, repetitive creature that we are—into someone who begins repeating thoughts and behaviors, strongly holding beliefs as true or false, and fiercely needing their socks to be folded this way and not that way, and their eggs to be cooked this way and not that way.

How we get from some particular feature of original personality to a passion for three-minute eggs is anybody's guess. But that we get there indubitably happens. Original personality comes with all sorts of readinesses—from the readiness to write a novel, to the readiness to grow sad when a cloud passes in front of the sun—and over time, those readinesses coalesce into our formed self, an awfully stiff creature.

Our available personality can be thought of as our remaining freedom—our ability to apply awareness to our situation, penetrate our own defenses, and see exactly what we are up to. It is the part of us that can have a chat about whether a four-minute egg might prove just as lovely as a three-minute egg, whether we are drinking far too much alcohol, or whether there is anything we can do about our chronic sadness.

Your available personality is at your disposal to heal, change, and grow. It is rather more important that we form strong current intentions and then struggle to follow through on those intentions by employing our available personality, than try to fathom the contours of our original personality or comprehend how exactly our readinesses led to the person we currently are. That is, it is really useful to focus on who we want to be and dream up ways of using our available personality to achieve those goals.

Each time you do more of this work of redesigning your mind, you enter your mindroom a freer person. The room is changing by virtue of your redesign and redecoration efforts, but so is the you who is arriving there. Picture that! Both you and the room are changing.

We come with an original personality about which we will never know enough, a formed personality that amounts to our rote, mechanical ways of operating, and an available personality that amounts to our remaining freedom. This simple construction allows for a really generous world of complexity. On a given day, we may be pulled by our original personality in ways that perplex us, disturb us, and even derail us. Some sudden urge may war with our formed personality.

But we get to employ our available personality and say, "Wow, what a tumultuous day! Still, I can go about my business of living my life purposes, as that's what's most important!"

This focus on available personality and the effort to make use of it returns us to the vibrant present, where the project of our life is actively worked on. Of course, the amount of available personality at our disposal changes. It is never a precise or a static amount but rather, a contextual amount. We quite naturally have more of it available in situations that promote freedom, and less of it available in situations that restrict our freedom.

For example, you may basically be a compassionate person. But if you're suddenly thrust into the role of "prison guard"— as students were who participated in a well-known social psychological experiment conducted at Stanford—you may find your compassion flying right out the window. Some usually well-managed bit of sadism from deep inside may suddenly erupt at such a moment. Yes, that is terribly disconcerting, but that is also the truth of the matter.

This metaphor of a tripartite personality can prove really useful to you. It gives you an elegant way of speaking to yourself about freedom and personal responsibility. It allows you to say the following: "Was I born sad, or maybe born ready to become sad? That's possible. So that's going to amount to a lifelong challenge. And I'm free to figure out what to do about that." And you are! You enter your mindroom, use the tactics we've been discussing, make use of your available personality to, for instance, remove your heavy winter overcoat and let in a summer breeze, and operate as the freest possible version of yourself.

· + ○ + ·

Visualization: Visualize yourself making use of your available personality to upgrade your formed personality.

Writing Prompt: Play with the metaphor of original personality, formed personality, and available personality. Where, for instance, are you least free or most locked into your formed personality? How might you apply your available personality to make a change there?

PART IV

PRACTICES AND CELEBRATIONS

THE PRACTICE OF SPEAKING: YOUR SPEAKER'S CORNER

In Part IV, I describe several practices that will improve your indwelling and your life. I believe that the practices I describe ought to be regular practices—better yet, daily practices, because the habit of daily practice does a much better job of redesigning your mind than does doing something irregularly or intermittently. Imagine sitting on your easy chair only one day out of the month. What will those other twenty-nine days feel like?

The same goes for anything beneficial to you: if you only do it once in a while, what's going on the rest of the time? An important part of redesigning your mind involves instituting and maintaining daily practices that are solid and helpful.

The first practice we'll examine is the practice of speaking your mind.

Freud suspected that all cases of writer's block were instances of self-censorship. It wasn't that the writer didn't have words or ideas, but that they were afraid to express and share them for some reason.

Self-censorship is a huge issue for all human beings (creatives, of course, definitely included). This truth helps explain why public speaking is the world's number one phobia: most people are made profoundly anxious by having to speak in public and reveal something about themselves. Even if what they have to say has nothing to do with them personally, they are still revealing how well or how poorly they organize their thoughts, make sense, look competent, and so on. Their presentation may be about sales statistics, but *they* are on full display. Think of how true this is for a research scientist considering presenting a controversial theory, a painter contemplating a suite of antisocial paintings, or an author thinking about writing a novel with a theme of revenge.

At such times, what are we afraid we might reveal? That we aren't as smart as we'd like to think we are. That we aren't as talented. That we aren't as accomplished. That our performance leaves a lot to be desired. That our writing is uninspired. That our visual imagery is trite. That we're second rate. That we're derivative. That we're somehow disgusting. That we're behind the times. That we're childish. That we're... you name it.

It can feel frankly unsafe to say what's on your mind. To make a political or social statement in a blog post, essay, book, song, or painting is to invite pushback, criticism, ruptures, and retaliation, as well as real financial, familial, and job consequences—in many places and times, even imprisonment or death. It is completely reasonable to take seriously the consequences of speaking your mind. But taking those consequences seriously and deciding never to speak again are two different things. The first is prudence; the second is abject silence.

What can help? A dedicated speaker's corner in the room that is your mind.

Historically, the most famous speaker's corner was the northeast corner of Hyde Park in London. But there are many other literal speaker's corners, both in England and around the world: in Indonesia, the Netherlands, Italy, Canada,

Australia, Singapore, Thailand, and elsewhere. They provide a designated place for a person to speak their mind—though, contrary to popular belief, not all speech is permitted there. In the speaker's corner that you create in your mindroom, *all* speech is permitted.

Why might you be censoring yourself and not speaking? Well, you might be a Charles Darwin, worried about how your naturalistic views might be received in a dangerously religious environment. You might be a Francisco Goya, worried about how your activist paintings might be received in an authoritarian environment. You might be a James Baldwin, worried about how your homoerotic writings might be received in a virulently homophobic environment. Whatever the source of your self-censorship happens to be, you don't want to censor yourself before you've had a chance to speak your mind, at least to yourself. Use your speaker's corner to practice the daily speaking of all things dangerous and unmentionable.

How might you design your speaker's corner? Will it be an old-fashioned soap box with a megaphone? A podium with a microphone? A spotlighted stage and a hand mic? Where will you put it? Will you position it in a far corner of your mindroom, or in some more prominent spot?

Give those details some thought right now as you situate and design your speaker's corner. Then try it out! Visualize yourself standing there and speaking your truth. Picture yourself eloquent, forthright, and powerful. How might you use your speaker's corner? What do you hear yourself saying?

Say that you've been writing a novel and for some reason you've gotten stuck. You might be blocked for any number of reasons, but one may be self-censorship. Go to your speaker's corner and speak your novel's darkest, most difficult truths. See how they sound out loud. Are they indeed dark and difficult but not as dangerous-feeling as you imagined them to be? Or do they reveal too much about you and therefore really must be avoided and excluded? Do your brave speaking, do your equally brave evaluating, and see what you've learned.

Maybe you'll be able to immediately resume writing your novel. Maybe you'll have learned how to revise it strategically. Maybe you'll understand why it must be abandoned. The chances are excellent that your courageous efforts at speaking will have produced some useful movement.

Create a speaker's corner in the room that is your mind. Use it to speak your mind and help eliminate self-censorship.

· ✦ ○ ✦ ·

Visualization: Visualize a speaker's corner in your mindroom and visualize yourself going there every day to speak some important, dangerous-feeling truth that has been hard to admit.

Writing Prompt: Write on the question, "What do I find really hard to say?"

THE PRACTICE OF DEVOTION: YOUR ALTAR

Most human beings are not as disciplined as they would like to be (again, creatives included). They do, naturally enough, bad-mouth themselves about that lack of discipline. But discipline may not be the issue. It is just as likely—perhaps even more so—that the issue may be a lack of devotion. There is a devotional quality to creativity, a deep regard for and love of the work that allows a creator to continue creating day in and day out, even when life is hard and the work is recalcitrant. If that devotion isn't there, resistance and blockage are likely to follow.

Italian operatic singer Luciano Pavarotti once explained:

> "People say I am disciplined. It is not discipline. It is devotion. There is a great difference."

There *is* a big difference. Discipline is an excellent commodity, and anyone attempting to live their life-purpose choices and create or perform needs a good measure of it. But if you aren't also devoted to your own efforts, if you don't see their merits and value at a deeper level than mere utility or interest, it will prove very hard to spend a lifetime struggling with a tangled problem in physics, or to spend four years slogging through the writing and rewriting of a complex, unwieldy novel. Devotion as well as discipline is needed to pull off such feats.

What can help in this regard is a devotional altar that supports your intention to stay devoted to your work. For me, the idea of an altar has no particular spiritual connotations. Rather, it is a visual aid in support of our human abilities to love life and stand up for truth, beauty, and goodness. I respect and love humanist ideals and traditions and include a miniature Magna Carta as part of my mindroom altar, along with a postcard of a Paris café scene, and other objects and images that hold meaning for me. That internal altar helps keep me motivated.

Go to the room that is your mind and look around. Where might you place your altar? Will you put it on top of your dresser? Will you place it on your work desk? Will you place it on a plant stand next to your easel? Will you place it on the mantel above your fireplace, if the mantel is wide enough? And no reason why it can't be wide enough, given that you get to design it! Pick a location for your altar, one that will keep it very present in your consciousness.

Next, decide what your altar will include. It can include absolutely anything that connects to the devotion you feel for life and for your life-purpose efforts. You might include a dusty book from a bygone age, a handsome slide rule, a gloriously colorful photograph of a distant nebula, a miniature Bill of Rights, a relic from a meaningful trip you took, your daughter's baby shoes—anything at all. Arrange your altar exactly as you would like it to look, including how it's lit, and step back. Does it suit you?

Now experience it. Visualize yourself in front of it. Feel connected to your work. Feel connected to your traditions. Feel connected to your intentions. Feel connected to your personal, idiosyncratic, individualistic vision of life. Feel connected to whatever you consider important. Experience a feeling of devotion. Notice how distracting, disturbing, and pestering thoughts dissolve in the glow of this devotion. Feel suffused with the feeling of it.

Because your altar exists in your mindroom, you can change it whenever you like. Maybe on one visit it'll resemble a room in the British Library, and on another visit, you'll populate it with spring flowers. Maybe sometimes it'll have an ancient feel to it, and other times, a contemporary feel. You can conceptualize your altar either way: permanent, like a pilgrimage site, or changeable, like light changing throughout the day. What matters is that you feel devotion well up in you as you encounter it.

· ✦ ○ ✦ ·

Visualization: Visualize an altar where you go to pledge your devotion and experience the feeling of devotion.

Writing Prompt: To what are you pledging your devotion? See if you can articulate that.

THE PRACTICE OF PASSION: YOUR BLAZING FIRE

Although it might seem self-evident that a smart, sensitive, creative individual would feel naturally motivated to engage in their creative work, in reality, the majority of creatives and all would-be creatives find it hard to maintain motivation.

For one thing, the work is arduous and comes with knotty intellectual and creative challenges. For another, only a percentage of it will prove good, and an even smaller percentage excellent. For a third, whatever they produce is open to criticism, rejection, dismissal, pushback, and scrutiny. Indeed, it is much harder to maintain motivation when working creatively than one might imagine at first glance.

That motivation can even vanish entirely. An infant is motivated to cry when hungry. But if you consistently fail to attend to that baby, they will lose their motivation to cry, grow silent, fall into despair, "fail to thrive," and may even die. A lack of response to their cries saps their motivation to keep crying and can even sap their motivation to live. What if a novelist keeps sending out their first novel and no one will publish it? Can they maintain their motivation to send it out, or maintain their motivation to work on their second novel? Can *they* thrive?

That ignored infant loses their taste for living and their desire to live. A creative person can lose their taste for creating, their desire to create, and even their desire to live, for a long laundry list of reasons. Therefore, it is on their shoulders to pay attention to this issue of motivation and find ways to maintain it in the face of that long laundry list of challenges. When that flame starts to dwindle, they must pay attention to that dwindling and stoke the fire. If that fire goes out completely, they must relight and rekindle it.

Whatever else they do in order to rekindle their desire to create, it would be smart if they also installed a fireplace in their mindroom, built a blazing fire, and warmed themselves there. At some deep level that connects to our primitive instincts, a blazing fire in a fireplace means something to us. It sparks our imagination as much as it warms our hands and feet. Your mindroom ought to have one.

Keeping a fire perpetually lit in that fireplace, moving their easy chair near it, and warming themselves there are among a creative person's most important tasks. To the extent that they are cold and unmotivated, exactly to that extent will they experience tenacious creative blocks and massive resistance to creating. Rather than bad-mouthing themselves or pestering themselves as to why they are not creating, the better plan is for them to announce, "I'm feeling cold and unmotivated—a fire will help!"

They can use that blazing fire in other ways as well. It is the place where they can write out their regrets on small pieces of paper and burn them. They can burn rejection letters from literary agents or gallery owners who refused to represent them. They can read the memoir they're working on by the light of that blazing fire. They can daydream and fantasize there. It is the place that makes their easy chair feel all that much cozier, while serving as a powerful reminder that motivation can wax, wane, and even die out—and they mustn't let that happen.

Picture the room that is your mind. You have an easy chair already installed. Now, install your fireplace opposite it. Have an ample supply of logs available. Have plenty of kindling. Start a lovely fire and begin to enjoy it. Announce to yourself, "This fire warms me, motivates me, and enables me to get on with my work." Sit for a while, enjoying the beauty and the warmth of your fire. Then, move to your desk or your easel and launch into your work.

When desire wanes, it's hard to face our creative work. When that spark dies completely, facing it feels almost impossible. You can keep the flame of desire alive in all sorts of ways, but one useful way is to install a fireplace in the room that is your mind, keep a fire blazing there, and demand of yourself that you'll never let it die out.

· ✦ ○ ✦ ·

Visualization: Visualize a fireplace hosting a blazing fire. Use this fire to rekindle your desire to live your life purposes and to attend to your creative work.

Writing Prompt: In addition to warming yourself by this blazing fire, what else will you do when your motivation wanes?

THE PRACTICE OF MEANING-MAKING: YOUR MEANING FOUNTAIN

As I discussed in an earlier chapter, meaning is a certain sort of psychological experience. Therefore, like all psychological experiences, it comes and goes. The bad news is that it can go, but the good news is that it can come back. We can have the experience of meaning again, especially if we actively "make meaning" by engaging in activities that we previously experienced as meaningful, and if we make sure to live our life purposes and our values.

Since meaning can and does return, the following is also true about meaning: it is a deep, inexhaustible wellspring and an infinitely renewable resource. Today it may not seem meaningful to sit by the pond and feed the ducks, as you have too much you want to do. Forty years from now—or tomorrow, for that matter—you may experience sitting by the pond for an hour or two as abundantly meaningful. An experience that felt meaningless one day can and may feel meaningful the next day. Meaning is like that.

To think of meaning as something to seek, search for, or find—something like a lost wallet or a lost ring—is to picture meaning as a very paltry thing. In that model, meaning is so small a commodity that you can acquire it just by attending a guru's lecture. You weren't sure what was meaningful in life, then a guru tells you, and now you know. Really? I hope that you're not holding meaning as that sort of thing.

No, meaning is nothing like that and nowhere out there. If it were, that would make it a tiny, trivial sort of thing. What if you were informed by a booming voice that the meaning of life was to stand on one foot while singing show tunes? Would that impress you or work for you? I hope not.

Bob, a client, explained to me:

> "I know nothing about ultimate reality, and I'm certain that no one else does either. But I recognize that some things feel meaningful to me, even consistently meaningful. If this is true, that is the same thing as saying that meaning is available to me. It may not be available to me at all times, in all moods, or in all weather, but I embrace the idea that meaning is a renewable human resource. More than that, I can take charge of it bubbling up. This may sound strange in words, but I know what I mean. I know how to accomplish this feat of restoring the meaning flow in my life."

Marcia, another client, explained to me:

> "As I began to really see that meaning is a wellspring, I felt more connected, hopeful, and empowered. I felt a sense of not only connecting to particular meaning-making choices, but to a deeper awareness of the limitlessness of possible meanings and choices. I found myself at times visualizing journeying into a

wellspring deep in the earth, traveling through time, traveling and shape-shifting into the awareness and viewpoints of other people, of animals, of trees, of energies that had taken a drink from the wellspring. They were like little creation stories. As soon as I internally agreed that meaning was a wellspring it not only shifted my understanding of meaning-making, but brought on a lightness as well."

Susan, yet another client, put it this way:

"Conceptualizing meaning as a wellspring changed my relationship to meaning. Like Old Faithful, the famous Yellowstone geyser, I began arriving at my desk with a bubbling up of energy. I experienced a building sense of creativity during the days when, because of my other responsibilities, I couldn't get to my writing. Then, on the days when I could, I found myself able to stay put for much longer periods of time. The image of an inexhaustible wellspring helped me maintain meaning on the days when I couldn't get to the computer, and it helped me make meaning on the days when I could. It seemed to work on many levels, deepening my connection to my creative work, banishing existential depression, and helping me do ordinary, everyday things more lightly and effortlessly."

Let's do the following. Let's add a courtyard right outside your mindroom. In that courtyard, install a burbling fountain. Decide on its look: maybe it looks like a Roman fountain, a fountain you might find in Seville, or some whimsical Calderesque fountain. This fountain is a meaning wellspring and reminds you that meaning is an inexhaustible resource. If you are having a boring day, a sad day, or a meaningless day, head directly to that shady courtyard and sit by your meaning fountain. Enjoy the play of light on water and feel meaning return.

· ✦ ○ ✦ ·

Visualization: Visualize a courtyard and a fountain. Sit beside your fountain and experience meaning returning.

Writing Prompt: Write on the following question: "If life only feels meaningful when I experience it as meaningful, what does that suggest?"

THE PRACTICE OF TEMPERATURE REDUCTION: YOUR BUCKET OF ICE WATER

The inside of a human being is a roiling place that can produce terrible impulses and even the occasional monster. We call all that roiling wildness our primitive nature, and we suppose that it arises from some ancient, less refined part of our brain, some place of lizards and caveman solutions. But who can say? Maybe it came from just yesterday, or even from this very morning. Are we really so civilized?

How does this roiling manifest? You may be thinking a very ordinary thought, like "Do I want butter or cream cheese on my bagel?" and right under that thought, a sea of a hot lava is boiling. It's ready to cascade out as a terrible episode of binge drinking, a truly careless affair that sends your whole life reeling, a horrible remark that you can never take back, or a violent gesture that no apology will ever make right. Or, strange to say, it may even manifest as a slovenly day of pajamas, fig bars, and television. To contain our hot lava, sometimes we become couch potatoes. How odd we are!

That lava is boiling in each of us, fiery red and hot as hell, which makes our mind a room built on top of an active volcano. Each of us lives in that danger zone. Can you sense that hot lava boiling even as you try to decide between butter and cream cheese for your bagel? I think you can. I think you can sense its presence through the cracks and fissures of consciousness as it sizzles away, ready to erupt. That you can sense it is a great thing. That means that you can prepare for those eruptions. How? By keeping a bucket of ice water handy.

Picture your mindroom. Identify the spot where you'll keep your bucket of ice water. Maybe you'll place it directly beneath that still life painting of apricots, or next to the dresser where you keep your hat collection, your power bars, and your beauty mementos. Have it ready!

You sense a lava eruption—something wild and unwanted is about to happen. What to do? Grab your bucket of ice water and ready yourself. When those first red threads of molten lava appear, douse them with the ice water. What a steam bath you'll create! You'll have trouble seeing and trouble breathing, but you will have instantly cooled the lava and turned it into black rock. You'll have created your own version of Hawaii's Big Island. Isn't that a lovely thought, that you can transform your boiling insides into a tropical paradise just like that?

Even if you don't quite produce paradise, you will have prevented an escapade that might have cost you your marriage, your liver, or your self-respect. You cooled down your desire for revenge to an ember, accomplishing something good for your system. Yes, you had to tolerate some steam. Yes, that red glow was beautiful. Yes, you may actually prefer fire to ice. But the cost of letting that lava flow in is terrible self-scorching.

Do the following right now. Situate a bucket of ice water in your mindroom. You can keep it off in a corner if you like, so that it isn't obtrusive. But don't hide it behind that huge stuffed tiger or that pile of unread books. You want to be able to see it and know that it is there. Yes, a fire extinguisher doesn't add much to a room's décor, and likewise, your ice water bucket won't prettify your mind. But the goal isn't elegance. The goals are safety and self-respect.

We do not respect ourselves if we let hot lava rule. We can explain our behavior to ourselves after the fact ("I had this terrible impulse, I just couldn't control myself") but that's a little late, isn't it? Wouldn't it have been better to douse that impulse with ice water when it was just a red glow peeking through the floorboards?

· + ○ + ·

Visualization: Visualize a bucket of ice water that you employ to douse your dangerous primitive, hot-blooded impulses.

Writing Prompt: Which monsters inhabit you?

THE PRACTICE OF EMOTIONAL RELEASE: YOUR POINTER FINGER

We have the sense that thoughts reside in the mind, whose location seems to be in our head. But where do feelings reside?

It would be nice if feelings had their own room. If they had a room like the one that is our mind, we could do similar work on them. We might install windows in that room, get a second easy chair, and so on. That would be lovely and helpful. But we don't seem to experience feelings in that same way.

So let's employ a different metaphor for feelings. Rather than imagining that they reside in a room, which doesn't feel true, let's imagine that they circulate in our system, the way that the air circulates in our house when we turn on the heat or the air conditioning. In fact, feelings seem to circulate like that, coursing through our bloodstream and our nervous system.

Sometimes nothing in particular seems to be coursing through us and we feel rather neutral. If asked, we might say, "I'm not feeling anything in particular." But then something happens—a small incident on the bus, a toe stub, a bad memory, a desire—and we can almost hear that *swoosh* of a feeling suddenly beginning to circulate. It's as if the heat suddenly came on, raising our inner temperature by ten or twenty degrees.

The anger. The sadness. The humiliation. The flooding of feelings that just about knock us off our feet. And why shouldn't feelings affect us exactly that powerfully, if they are suddenly flowing everywhere in our system, into every nook and cranny of our being? How those feelings rush everywhere, overwhelming thought and completely kidnapping the moment!

But isn't that image of a feeling coursing everywhere suggestive of what you might do to deal with it? What if, instead of giving it permission to flow everywhere, you could isolate that coursing feeling a little bit? Think of a smart house with individual temperature zones, one where you can make your bedroom toasty without having to heat the whole house. What if you could do that with feelings?

Imagine that you could isolate that bad feeling that just welled up in you—isolate it, say, in the index finger of your left hand. When the feeling courses through you, mentally send it in the direction of your left hand and funnel it into your left index finger. Having done that excellent isolating, your finger is the now the only place where you're feeling that feeling. Isn't that already an improvement?

But you could do even more. You could use your index finger like a pistol and shoot that feeling at some imaginary target, releasing it from your system. Or you might use your index finger like a pen and scrawl graffiti on some imaginary brick wall, writing away the feeling. Or you might use your index finger like an eyedropper and let the bile drip out, drop by bilious drop, into the sink. Or you might use your imagination to dream up another sort of cleansing ritual to do with your pointer finger, now that you've mindfully and carefully isolated that bad feeling.

Practice by starting with a small emotion, like a minor bit of irritation. Maybe you've just missed your train. How frustrating! Stop. Breathe. Aim that feeling of irritation that's coursing through your system toward your left index finger. Fire that emotion at the departing train pulling out of the station. As the train vanishes, so does the irritation!

Move on to a middle-sized emotion. You have a chat with one of your parents and get criticized. Okay. Here comes the emotion. *Whoosh!* It's everywhere, racing through your arteries and veins. Breathe. Yes, this is harder, but try. Aim that anguish and anger toward your left index finger. Maybe say something out loud, like "Get moving, you bad feeling!" Take that now-isolated feeling to the sink and, using your pointer finger like an eye dropper, rid yourself of your pain and resentment.

Let's try a big emotion. We'll need to be very careful here. Big emotions are *big*. They can be horribly painful, maddeningly intense, even overwhelming. Breathe several times. Try to angle this big emotion toward your left index finger. This may prove much harder, but try. Corral it there. That's a lot of emotion for one finger! But maybe you managed. Okay, now... get rid of it. Maybe use it as ink to draw a ferocious drawing that you then burn in your fireplace.

You will need more tactics than just this one to deal with your emotions. Spend a little time and dream up some additional fanciful, provocative, amazing strategies for dealing with the emotions that rise up in us every day. You don't want to do a wonderful job of minding your thoughts, and at the same time, skip minding your feelings. We've been working on dynamically self-regulating your thoughts. What about dynamically self-regulating your feelings as well? Isn't that an excellent idea?

· + ○ + ·

Visualization: Visualize yourself with the power to send negative feelings in the direction of your left index finger and then expel them right out of your system.

Writing Prompt: How can you use the metaphor of "the room that is your mind" to better deal with negative and painful feelings?

Redesign Your Mind

THE PRACTICE OF RESILIENCE: YOUR REBOUND CORNER

Our feelings get hurt regularly, often on a daily basis. We may pride ourselves on our rationality, but how can we think clearly if our feelings have been hurt? How can we live our life purposes and try to make meaning if our wounded feelings burden us too heavily? Mustn't it be one of our more profound life tasks to rebound from hurt feelings and upgrade our resilience, or else risk having those hurt feelings rob us of life?

Consider Mary. A painter, she sent her slides off to a gallery where she had high hopes for representation. What she got back was the terse email: "You are such an amateur!" Mary stopped painting for the next three years and didn't resume until we began working together. Such dramatically negative events happen all too often in the lives of creatives. One sharp criticism can derail an artist for far too long—sometimes forever—making them completely doubt that they have the right or the wherewithal to be a professional artist, or any artist at all.

The consequences of receiving a blow of this sort last so long, in part because our initial reaction to them is huge and outsized, like an explosion going off. When someone says to you, either in veiled language or in no uncertain terms, that you are an idiot, that you have no talent, that you're a fool, that you're mediocre, that you're a hack, that you're derivative, that you're...fill in the blank...you *will* have a reaction—a fierce, whole-body, emotional reaction that can shift your worldview and your very identity.

Virtually everyone has these powerful, visceral reactions to being criticized, humiliated, or shamed. These reflexive reactions, like our blushing response or our fight-or-flight response, are fundamental, hard-wired parts of who we are. Maybe some very advanced, very detached, or very defended human being can avoid feeling the sting of these blows, but the rest of us *will* feel them. It will physically feel as if a huge, bad event has happened. And yet, all that has *really* happened is that we are having a feeling.

After the initial pain subsides, what are you going to do next? Now the ball is in your court. What you do next may affect how you experience the next year, or even the rest of your life. What to try? Create a corner in your mindroom, a rebound corner, where you'll go immediately when a powerful negative feeling strikes. When you get to your rebound corner, acknowledge that something large-feeling has happened. Recognize that you suddenly find yourself awash in stress hormones, negative thoughts, and painful feelings. At the same time, *reject that anything really important has happened.*

Alert yourself to the fact that you are just feeling a feeling. You may only be able to do this after the initial pain has subsided, but after those first few seconds or few minutes, you may be able to whisper, "Wow, that was a big feeling." Breathe. Then murmur, "Sooner rather than later." This is your rebound mantra that signifies your intention to get over this feeling as soon as humanly possible.

Once the pain has subsided, leave your rebound corner, settle yourself in your easy chair, and bravely engage in an assessment of the situation. That assessment might sound like: "Darn, I hated being told that my paintings were dead!

But I see how trying to copy my really lifelike photographic collages onto the canvas has produced fairly dead paintings. I've known that for a while. Okay, now I fully accept that truth. I can't do that sort of painting any longer." Once you've used your rebound corner to deal with the initial pain, take to your easy chair and decide what to make of the accusation.

You might want to add a resilience mat to your rebound corner. Picture a yoga mat, a gym mat, or any sort of mat you like. Stretch out on this mat, grow calm, feel resilience flow throw your system, and arrive at a place of renewed power. To get there, you may have to forgive your critic, forgive yourself, or even forgive the universe for dealing you such blows. This was the case for Lars, a coaching client. Lars explained:

"I need to forgive everything. I have a tendency to immerse myself in too many facts about the world, bringing weight, inertia, and opacity to my reality. All that heaviness makes it almost impossible to act or to create. It has dawned on me that an all-encompassing forgiveness is the first step in dissolving my heavy reality and opening myself up to creativity. I must forgive everything, so that my laboriously collected thoughts, experiences, sorrows, rules, habits, perceived limits, etc., are liberated. I understand this liberation as a form of generosity in my relationship with myself."

We are obliged to muster resilience in the face of all sorts of challenges—poor health, relationship difficulties, creative missteps, hurricanes, meaning crises, and all the rest. A powerful step in rebounding is ceremonially picking ourselves up off the mat. To do that, it can help to create that mat. Add a resilience mat to your rebound corner and practice rebounding quickly from life's many blows.

· ✦ ○ ✦ ·

Visualization: Visualize a rebound corner where you go to recover quickly from psychological blows.

Writing Prompt: What might help increase your resilience?

THE PRACTICE OF RELATIONSHIP: YOUR APPOINTMENT CALENDAR

Relationships can prove problematic for everyone, and maybe especially for smart, sensitive, creative individuals who struggle to retain their individuality, who jealously guard their solitude, and who find their healthy narcissism mixed with a good-sized dose of unhealthy narcissism.

Indeed, creatives may even be constitutionally primed to go it alone. Still, if you don't foster relationships, it's harder to achieve emotional health and a measure of happiness. Even if relating isn't your first choice, it would be wise if it were a close second.

Creatives regularly forget that relating is also important. By forgetting to relate, they can become isolated, lonely, and sad. A tactical solution to this common problem is to create an appointment calendar that you keep and maintain in the room that is your mind. Its literal counterpart is also necessary, where you make your actual appointments. But you'll also want to keep one in your mindroom as a talisman and as a reminder that relating is something vital to you.

Let's imagine that it's a dull, unexceptional day, that life feels a bit drab, and that some sadness is dogging your heels. That might prove the perfect moment to visit your mindroom, pull out your appointment calendar from the desk drawer where you keep it, and wonder, "Who would I like to see?" Let the people you know parade in front of you. Maybe include people you don't know yet but whom you'd enjoy meeting. Let that parade unfold.

Think about each person in turn. Aunt Lilly. Cousin Tony. The woman you met at the art opening who got your jokes and shared your enthusiasms. That friend from high school who holds some oddly important place in your memory. Your daughter who, now that she is working in the next town, you rarely see. That expert in your field who you suppose would never deign to have a cup of coffee with you—but who knows? That editor who once almost published a book of yours. Your neighbor two doors down who always waves. Your father...well, that may be a tricky one.

Maybe your answer will surprise you. Maybe it will turn out that you would really like to visit with Aunt Lilly because she, more than anyone else in the family, likes to recount family history—and it's a bit of family history that you're craving. Maybe you'll discover that you want to reach out to that expert—and more than that, you want to propose a collaboration. Maybe it will suddenly occur to you that the editor who almost bought that book from you genuinely loved your writing style—and your new book may be right up their alley. Who knows at what face in the parade you'll stop?

You might engage with your appointment calendar in conjunction with some other ceremony. For instance, you might pull out your life-purpose china, choose the relationship plate, and have a nice snack on it while perusing that people parade. If someone's face brings up a bitter memory, you might try tolerating that pain for a full ten seconds while wondering if there's something new to learn

about that old story. You might begin by throwing open the
windows you've installed and letting a fresh breeze blow away
any stray anxiety that might be building as you think about
these various people, each with their own warts and shadows.
Then...make some appointments.

How many creative people have suffered because they could
not or would not love, and could not or would not enjoy the
company of others? Don't number yourself among those
many. The appointment calendar that you maintain in your
mindroom can help you remember that human contact
is important.

· ✛ ✚ ✛ ·

Visualization: Visualize an appointment calendar
that you use to help you maintain contact
with others.

Writing Prompt: Discuss the pluses and minuses
of relating.

THE PRACTICE OF IDENTITY: YOUR IDENTITY PLEDGE

Say that you intend to be a filmmaker. That means that you are obliged to internally identify as a filmmaker. If you don't identify as a filmmaker—if you don't raise your hand when someone says, "Who in the room is a filmmaker?"—you're that much less likely to actually make films.

It's crucial that you add the identity of filmmaker to all of the other identity pieces that you may possess—your identity as a woman, a Jew, a Bostonian, a Francophile, an opera lover, and so on. A way to do this? Create the identity pledge "I am a filmmaker!" Murmur it as you enter your mindroom, then shout it out like a warrior's cry when you leave.

Give this a try right now. Visualize entering your mindroom and murmuring "I am a filmmaker," or whatever identity piece you intend to put front and center.

In addition to employing your identity pledge, make sure to do all of the following practices. These will help you strengthen your identity as a filmmaker (or any identity piece you need to strengthen):

- Get in the habit of publicly saying "I am a filmmaker." Just as it is powerful and useful for an alcoholic to say, "I am an alcoholic" publicly and out loud at an AA meeting, it is likewise powerful and useful for a filmmaker (even one who hasn't made films yet) to say publicly "I am a filmmaker." When someone asks you what you do, say "I'm a filmmaker" rather than "I sell shoes at Macy's." There is a world of difference in these two ways of identifying yourself. The first allows you to think about film, talk about film, network about film, and *be* a filmmaker. The second does no such thing.

- Prepare answers to those questions that, when put to you, cause you to lose your will to call yourself a filmmaker. One such question might be: "Have you made any films yet?" A second question might be: "Would I have seen any of your films?" A third might be: "Do you make full-length films or just shorts?" Bravely articulate the questions that bother you, embarrass you, weaken you, or stop you, and then create your answers. For instance, to the question "Have you made any films yet?" your prepared answer might be: "I'm working on one right now on the theme of immigration—care to invest in it?" That'll turn the tables, won't it?

- Notice if and when your filmmaker identity begins to weaken or vanish. This happens characteristically when you've spent too much time not operating as a filmmaker—as months go by and you neither plan nor make films. During those sad months, it is entirely likely that you begin to think of yourself less and less as a filmmaker. You want to notice that this is happening, even though it is painful to notice. Admit to yourself that your identity is eroding and engage in self-talk that boosts your identity back up.

- Know what to do when you think you've lost your right to call yourself a filmmaker—because you haven't made a film in five years, because your last film was roundly panned, because you have to pay to make your films yourself, etc. Over none of these events should you lose your right to call yourself a filmmaker. That can only happen if you let it happen. When you feel as if you've lost that right, what will you do? At the very least, resume saying "I am a filmmaker!" both internally and publicly. Know *exactly* what you're going to do when you feel your right to call yourself a filmmaker slipping away.

- *Do* the various things that a filmmaker does. This means more than just the obvious "make films." It means understanding how films get made, from both a technical and financial standpoint. It means forming working relationships with people who can help you. It means learning to use language in rhetorically strong ways so that you can make your films sound interesting to investors and audiences. It means understanding how to audition actors and work with casting directors. It means wooing rich people and learning how to negotiate the monied class. It means engaging in apprenticeship activities that serve you. These are the sorts of things that filmmakers do. To solidify your self-identification as a filmmaker, you will want to do them, too!

- Make supporting your filmmaker identity a daily practice by paying attention to it morning, noon, and night—even every time you enter your mindroom. Maybe that should become a password phrase that allows you entry into your mindroom: "I am a filmmaker." There may be days when you don't work on your film, but there should be no days when you don't identify as a filmmaker.

You want daily contact with your filmmaker identity. You want to know on a daily basis whether or not you are manifesting that identity, and if you aren't manifesting it, you want to take some immediate action. *Be* a filmmaker every day and *support your identity* of filmmaker every day. Your identity pledge can help!

· ✦ ○ ✦ ·

Visualization: Visualize entering your mindroom and murmuring "I am a filmmaker," or whatever identity piece needs strengthening.

Writing Prompt: Pick one of your identities that you feel needs attention. How will you attend to it?

CHAPTER 55

THE PRACTICE OF FOCUS: YOUR CORRECTIVE LENSES

Creatives often lose focus when they tackle a particular creative project or intellectual problem. They start with great enthusiasm on a given novel, certain in their bones that they know what the novel is all about. Then, even after just a few days, it becomes much less clear to them what they're doing. The plot has morphed, important characters have lost their significance, minor characters are wanting to take over, and the setting is demanding a shift from one continent to another. Suddenly, the very reason for writing this novel has dimmed to near invisibility. The project has gone completely out of focus.

At this point, there is a great temptation to abandon the project, which can leave a creative with a million begun things and no completed ones. To abandon a project merely because it is morphing and has gone out of focus is to abandon it too soon. To embrace the phrase that is now wanting to well up—"I have no idea what's going on!"—as a reason to abandon the project, rather than to accept all this morphing as a natural feature of the creative process, is to misunderstand the nature of process. Too many creatives, and virtually all would-be creatives, over-agitated by all that morphing, abandon their work too soon.

We can lose focus for other reasons as well. Maybe some other project becomes insistent and asks—demands—to be worked on, causing our current project to dim and grow vague. Maybe we have to turn away from our highly personal current project in order to tackle some creative work with commercial viability, so as to pay the bills. Maybe our health, a serious challenge with one of our children, or the state of the world grabs our attention. The ways in which current creative projects can dim, lose their luster, and shift out of focus are legion.

What can help you stay focused on your current project even as it morphs, even as you're pulled away from it by life and by other projects? One solution is to keep a set of eyeglasses with corrective lens on the side table next to your easy chair. The moment you put these eyeglasses on, your current project is brought back into focus.

First, you'll see its name in sharp, crystal-clear lettering. Of course, that means that your project needs a name. The name you employ need not be its perfect name or its final name, just a placeholder that, when seen clearly through those corrective lenses, brings your project flooding back to mind.

Having a solid working name for your project helps you remember it, picture it, understand it, and maintain motivation as you work on it. You might want to think that through right now and see if you can give your current project a solid working title, then try the following experiment. Let the project blur a bit. Put on your corrective eyeglasses. Experience the project returning in sharp focus. How exciting is that?

Use these special eyeglasses with corrective lenses to keep you on target throughout the course of a project—from its inception to its entry into the world. When a project grows blurry and loses focus, go directly to the room that is your mind, put on your glasses with their corrective lenses, and watch your project return instantly.

· ✦ ○ ✦ ·

Visualization: Visualize a pair of eyeglasses with corrective lenses that you employ to keep your important projects in focus.

Writing Prompt: What do you typically do when you lose focus on a creative project?

THE PRACTICE OF BOLDNESS: YOUR SEVEN-WORD CORNER

A painter came to see me. She explained that her husband, who had recently retired, kept visiting her in her studio to chat about inconsequential matters. I asked her to craft a sentence of seven words or fewer that communicated what she wanted to say to him about the preciousness of her painting time and her painting space.

Her first efforts were grotesquely long, apologetic, and weak. Finally, after many tries, she arrived at: "I can't chat while I'm working."

"Can you say that to him?" I asked.

"Yes," she replied.

"How does that feel?" I continued.

"Very, very scary."

Next, we role-played a situation she was having with the fellow who did some printing work for her. He was the only person in her area equipped to do this printing work, and she liked both the work he did and his prices. But he was always inappropriate with her, saying things like "You know, I have feelings for you," and "Most husbands don't understand their artist wives."

"What do you want to say to him?" I asked.

Having just practiced, she was now quicker to arrive at a strong response.

"I need you to stop that," she said. "I am coming here to have prints made, period." She laughed. "That's two sentences, and the second one's a little long. But that's the idea, right?"

"That's exactly the idea," I agreed.

You manifest your confidence by saying strong, clear things. Saying them in seven words or fewer is a great practice. Here are some examples of responses of seven words or fewer that a person is unlikely to make unless they've done a bit of practicing. The phrases I have in mind are in bold.

- Someone drops you an email saying that they love your work, though they can't afford to buy any of it. Typically, you might reply with a "thank you" and leave it at that. The new, bolder you might reply, "Thank you. I wonder: **might you tell your friends about me?** I'd appreciate that!"

- You're at a party, you find yourself chatting with someone about your art, and you have your usual difficult time explaining what it is you paint. The effort to explain yourself exhausts you and you have the sense that you haven't done a very good job of it. In such situations, it isn't likely that you're going to find some bold note to end on. However, you indeed manage a bold note and say, "**Would you like to visit my studio?**" Rather than presuming that you've made a hash of your explanations, you propose a visit.

- Your sister asks if you can take over minding your aging mother since "you don't have a job." You could meekly agree and lose several years of your life, or you could say, "**My painting is real work.**" Then you might continue, "Let's work out something equitable among all us kids, since we all have jobs and lives."

- You meet someone who says that their blog for new mothers is very popular. You might reply, "Great!" or you might reply, "Great! **Might your peeps be interested in me?**" They'll probably say, "Gee, I don't know, offhand I wouldn't think so," to which you might reply, "Yes, I understand, but let me tell you why they just might be interested."

- You get an email from an artist you know announcing their participation in a group show. You could congratulate them, or you could congratulate them and also ask, "**Room for one more in the show?**"

- You read a blog post in an online magazine about something tangentially related to the subject matter you paint. You could nod to yourself and move on, or you could drop that blogger an email and say, "Loved your post on firehouses! My art is right up that alley! **Care to do a piece on me?**"

Not being bold makes everything harder. One way to practice boldness is to create and visit a seven-word corner in your mindroom. Spend some time there creating short, strong declarations for various occasions. Likewise, when you have the feeling that you're about to reply too meekly, take a mental moment, visit your seven-word corner, craft a bold reply, and return with it. You may be surprised to discover just how many opportunities to speak boldly are presented to you. Be sure to take them!

· ✦ ○ ✦ ·

Visualization: Visualize a corner of your mindroom where you go when you want to practice speaking powerfully.

Writing Prompt: Discuss the difference between saying things by way of short sentences versus saying them by way of long sentences.

THROWING A MIND PARTY

When was the last time you had a party in your mind?

When was the last time you entered that room that is your mind with a bouquet of balloons, put on some salsa music, and invited all those sad guests slumped here and there to get up and dance? When, that is, did you have some fun in your mind? Not very recently, I'm willing to bet.

We need more mind parties. Most days our mind is a workaday place, a gloomy place, a steam kettle, or a piston-driven engine, not a party venue. Wouldn't it be fun to decorate it? And order a cake? And select a playlist? And gather some games? Lots of games! Not just another round of solitaire, or a crossword puzzle, or a game of sudoku, but something lively, tumultuous and over the top. Like, for instance, mind spin the bottle...

Picture someone you've loved to kiss. Get that champagne bottle out of your mind fridge, spin it, and wherever it points, there he or she is! Permission to kiss granted! Spin it again—oh, now it's *that* person. Excellent. Can you do too much kissing at the party in your mind? Not hardly!

Or try this mind party favorite: invite everyone to tell a story. Select a theme—maybe a great childhood moment, a first travel adventure, or the experience of a starry night full of awe and wonder. Have the storytellers pass around a talking stick (or maybe a talking pretzel). Let anyone pass who is too shy or too entranced to speak. Thank each storyteller, and then bring out the cake!

Who will you invite? The lovely thing about a mind party is that no one will turn you down. Invite whomever you like and they will be there! Invite some couples who dance the tango. Invite a top expert in a field you'd love to learn. Invite a hero of yours. Invite an ancestor, maybe that one you've heard all those stories about, the one who trained horses or invented the cream puff. Invite different versions of yourself from different epochs. Invite a whole mime troupe, or some performance artists who'll wrap your mindroom in pink yarn. Mix and match to your heart's content! If anyone bores you or disappoints you, send them packing.

A fellow I know is writing a book about lightness. He believes that lightness will save us. We are all so heavy, he feels—we live so heavy, we communicate so heavy, we work so heavy, we even love heavy. Where is the lightness? Where are the marshmallows? Where are the giggles? Where are the summer afternoons? It appears that in order to have that lightness, we must create it. It is perhaps a bit of irony and more unfortunate heaviness that we must create lightness in order to have it. But so be it. Dance time!

You may have some objections. "Oh, a party in the mind is too silly. A party in the mind is too frivolous. A party in the mind is a bit of pathetic self-indulgence. A party in the mind is just too goofy. What's the point?" Well, a party in the mind isn't silly, frivolous, self-indulgent, goofy, or pointless. It's a golden opportunity to lighten up, smile, and get off that treadmill of medium-sized sorrow that each of us is treading daily.

Then there's that most objectionable of objections: that somehow you don't deserve it. As if because you've made some messes and tripped up here and there you aren't entitled to joy. What an idea! Who sold you that bill of goods? Imagine a child saying to themselves, "I am too bad to deserve a birthday party." Doesn't that make you want to weep? Never think such a thought again. Parties in the mind are our eternal birthright!

What's my favorite party to throw? It's a quote party where I invite my favorite quotes to visit. There's a Tchaikovsky quote about inspiration that I love, a Pavarotti quote about devotion, several Camus quotes (and whole passages), and, well, some of my own quotes, too, where I've turned a phrase that I'm happy to remember. I bring out the folding chairs, put up bunting, make cupcakes (quotes love cupcakes), and greet each quote at the door with a really heartfelt greeting, as they are quite cherished. What a lovely time we have!

Your mind needs more joy. Every mind does. A party may be just the ticket. Throw one soon and enjoy the festivities!

· + ○ + ·

Visualization: Visualize a really wonderful mind party.

Writing Prompt: Discuss—and figure out how to dismiss—any objections you may have to throwing yourself a mind party.

SHUTTING THE LIGHTS

No sleep, no mental health.

Nothing is a better predictor of poor mental health than a lack of sleep. And so many people are sleeping poorly these days! Why all this insomnia? Because folks are worrying and tormenting themselves around the clock.

Are you wide awake too much of the time in your mindroom? When the moon is full, are you still staring at it rather than sleeping? When it's two in the morning, are you tossing and turning, repeatedly glancing at the clock, pestering yourself with some thought? This is a serious problem. If your mind gets no chance to rest, it starts to sicken. Your mind needs its rest!

How can you get it some rest? You might count sheep. You might take some chemical, which might produce the effect you want but will likely come with profound side effects. One well-known actor pictured a red dot that he made larger and smaller and larger and smaller until he wore himself out. Maybe you have your own favorite tricks. Maybe it has to do with how you prop your pillows. Maybe it has to do with some special tea. Most everyone is trying something because most everyone is having trouble sleeping.

What else might you try? Ceremonially saying goodnight to everything in your mindroom. Say goodnight with the same affection that you said goodnight to your beloved stuffed animals when you were a child. Visit your mindroom and murmur: "Goodnight, easy chair." "Goodnight, blazing fire." "Goodnight, snow globes." "Goodnight, life-purpose china." "Goodnight, speaker's corner." Say a gentle goodnight to each and every thing, including that devilish worry hiding in the corner and that spider's web of dread hanging from the ceiling.

Say some special goodnights. Do you have a grandchild halfway across the globe who makes you smile when you think of them, but who also brings you pain because you see them so rarely? Wish them a special goodnight. Say, "I love you, grandchild. I wish I could see you more! But here I am hugging you, dearest. Goodnight, love."

Do you have a special pestering thought that's pestered you for all eternity—maybe the thought that you're just not talented enough to write your novel, or just not attractive enough to compete in the singles' world? Say a special goodnight to that thought. That special goodnight might sound like: "Enough about talent, mind. I love the idea for my novel. Let me just try to write it. Peace to you, sad thought. Goodnight to you, sad thought. Sleep tight!"

As you quiet yourself for sleep, be gentle, peaceful, and self-comforting. Be gentle with each object, worry, and memory. Be as peaceful as you can be. Sing lullabies. Listen for the sounds of sleep around you—the light snoring of vague memories, the rhythmic breathing of your kindness toward yourself, the whispers of dreams arriving. Be gentle, peaceful, and self-comforting as you tiptoe about shutting down your mind for the night.

If a good night's sleep eludes you too often, your mind will begin to wear down. You may become strange to yourself, edgy, paranoid, unlikeable, and miserable. Your mind really does need its rest. Tonight, if the moon is too bright and your thoughts are too pestering, try making the rounds in your mindroom and saying a sweet goodnight to anything still awake in there.

· ✛ ○ ✛ ·

Visualization: Visualize yourself saying goodnight to all the contents of your mindroom.

Writing Prompt: What might you try to help yourself sleep better?

CALM ELIZABETH

As you redesign your mind, you change. You think different thoughts, you handle situations differently, you monitor your thoughts and feelings more carefully, you react less impulsively, and you make better decisions and stronger choices.

Elizabeth was a client who had been struggling with anxiety and who had made a serious effort to redesign her mind. She upgraded her personality and transformed herself into a calmer person. She sent me the following email, as she wanted to share the fruits of the work she had been doing on herself:

> "This week was a very stressful week, full of many adrenaline-rushed moments. My five-year-old finished preschool three weeks ago, and my eight-year-old finished two weeks ago. I was still teaching up until this week, so I have been on a new routine and schedule getting the kids to camp and classes while still teaching every day; and we were scheduled to leave to visit family on Friday.
>
> "I needed to remain extremely organized to make sure that everything got completed on time. I had to tackle a new task every day: the laundry, cleaning out the refrigerator, cleaning out the fish tank, cleaning the house, and packing up everyone's clothes and items for the trip. I also needed to deliver the final to my college students on Thursday, grade all thirty-one essays (four pages each), and submit my final grades before leaving. And because the universe has an

amazingly funny sense of humor, I was scheduled for jury duty Tuesday, which I didn't immediately get out of and had to continue calling in on standby all day.

"Needless to say, it was an extremely stressful few days leading up to the day we were leaving. Thursday night as I went to bed late, I talked with my husband about our luggage and went to bed having completed everything. But on Friday morning, my husband interrupted my workout to ask about something we had decided on just a few hours earlier the night prior. He was presenting at a conference and was very stressed and seemed to be picking a fight. As he was venting, *somehow, I remained calm.*

"We normally drive ten hours to get to our family, but my husband was traveling the next weekend and I didn't want to make the trip by myself home, so we decided to fly. We were supposed to take a small charter plane to try it out. The idea behind the decision was that, for a family of our size, it was actually cheaper than flying from a large airport, and it would be easier to not have to worry about what to pack or about getting to the airport hours early. Since my husband was presenting at the conference Friday and wasn't able to fly out until Friday evening, that left me traveling with my two children and our dog.

"I managed to stay on top of everything and on Friday, I arrived early to pick up my kids from their morning camp class. I had a lovely amount of time before I needed to pick them up so I decided I was going to meditate in the car, but something told me to check my email first. I found out our flight was two hours delayed. I was supposed to arrive on time because I had planned to see my best friend from high school,

whom I hadn't seen in twenty years. Our flight being
delayed meant I wouldn't be able to see her, because
her husband for some odd reason decided to have
them leave for their family trip early. Though I was
extremely disappointed, *somehow, I remained calm.*

"I had planned on having lunch with my mom when
we arrived, but I changed course to have lunch at
home before we left for the airport. We were finally on
our way and getting excited when I again checked my
email, only to find out that our flight was canceled.
Upset, I called my husband. He called the credit card
company and learned that our travel insurance only
covered delayed flights and not canceled flights. As I
made my way to the charter airport, I was very upset—
rather, I *thought* that I was very upset. I told the kids
that I was really upset and that they needed to be
patient with me. I did lots of deep breathing in the
car and I discovered that I wasn't in fact really upset.
Somehow, I had remained calm.

"The ladies at the ticketing counter helped us get on
a new flight at the closest major airport, took care
of our transportation there, and helped pack up the
car. As we were leaving, one of the women thanked
me. She said I was so patient and understanding,
whereas everyone else had been screaming at them
all afternoon, saying that they had intentionally
ruined their lives. She even commented on how well-
behaved my children were. We ended up arriving
to my hometown, with my mom greeting us nine
hours after we initially were supposed to arrive. *And
I was calm.*

"I laughed when I saw my mom waiting for us and
she wondered why I had a smile on my face after

that ordeal. I told her all about the woman thanking me for remaining calm, and my mom laughed and responded, 'You?!' She was as shocked as I was. I am not normally the calm person, not in any situation. I am like Ferdinand the bull: I want to be left alone to smell the flowers, but when you sting me, I get out of control. Or at least, that is who I used to be. I couldn't explain any of this to my mom, but I did want to write to you. I think I have a new mind. But whether or not I do, I really did have this experience. And it was a first."

If you redesign your mind, change your indwelling style, engage in dynamic self-regulation, think thoughts that serve you, and hold the intention to shed unwanted emotions sooner rather than later, you will get results. Personality may be a mysterious affair, but the way to upgrade it is straightforward. You apply your awareness to your own mind and redesign it so that it serves and suits you better.

· ✦ ○ ✦ ·

Visualization: Visualize an upgraded version of yourself.

Writing Prompt: As we near the end, single out one of our guided visualizations to focus on. Why have you chosen it and how will you use it?

A NEW YOU

We are nearing the end of this book but not the end of your adventure in upgraded thinking and living. Here's where I hope you'll arrive and how I hope the new you will speak:

> "I can clearly picture 'the room that is my mind,' where I go to engage in thinking, musing, creating, fantasizing, problem-solving, and all matters mental. I can design it, I can make decisions about how I'll be when I'm there (like, for instance, calm), and I can make it a useful place, a pleasant place, and even a magical place.
>
> "I understand that this metaphor is at once serious and playful. It is serious in the sense that it allows for improved self-regulation and a healthier internal mental environment. It is playful in the sense that I can be as whimsical and as fanciful as I like in the way that I design that room and in the ways that I use it.
>
> "I understand that many times, I will be driven there by some pressure. Even if I'm driven there, I can still engage in self-regulation. If, say, I'm driven there by an unproductive obsession or by some manic energy, I will know what to do. I have all sorts of visualizations and tactics at the ready!
>
> "I understand that what's important is not just 'what I think' but the indwelling style I champion. I want to experience indwelling as if I were sitting in a comfy

easy chair rather than lying on a bed of nails. I want to experience indwelling as pressure-free rather than pressurized. I want to experience indwelling as airy and breezy rather than stuffy and stale. All of this, I can accomplish!

"Just as I can arrive at the room that is my mind of my own volition, I can also leave it of my own volition. I have an exit door! I understand that part of healthy indwelling is recognizing that I can overdo spending time in my mindroom and that what may be required is leaving. Maybe I'm brooding too much, straining too hard to come up with an answer, overthinking an issue, or creating too many agitating thoughts. There are countless reasons why I might need to leave—and I know how to exit easily!

"I can chat with myself, regulate myself, and serve my interests, including my interests in living my life-purpose choices, creating the psychological experience of meaning, and doing my intellectual and creative work. I am conceptualizing that relationship as taking place in the room that is my mind. I may not always be happy there, but I am often happy there, and I'm certainly proud to be using my brain in this healthy, helpful, and useful way!"

This is you at your creative best, your intellectual best, and your mentally healthiest. You've learned how to redesign your mind so that it is your best mind possible. Congratulations!

ABOUT THE AUTHOR

Eric Maisel, PhD, is the author of more than fifty books including *Why Smart People Hurt*, *Fearless Creating*, *Mastering Creative Anxiety*, and *The Van Gogh Blues*. Widely regarded as America's foremost creativity coach, he is a former psychotherapist, active creativity coach, and critical psychology advocate. Dr. Maisel writes the "Rethinking Mental Health" blog for *Psychology Today*, lectures nationally and internationally, and provides keynotes for organizations like the International Society for Ethical Psychology and Psychiatry and the American Mental Health Counselors Association.

Dr. Maisel facilitates workshops in locations like Paris, London, New York, Dublin, Prague, and Rome, has provided hundreds of print, radio, and television interviews, and has taught tens of thousands of students through his classes, workshops, and webinars. He can be found at www.ericmaisel. com and www.kirism.com and can be reached at ericmaisel@ hotmail.com.

Mango Publishing, established in 2014, publishes an eclectic list of books by diverse authors—both new and established voices—on topics ranging from business, personal growth, women's empowerment, LGBTQ studies, health, and spirituality to history, popular culture, time management, decluttering, lifestyle, mental wellness, aging, and sustainable living. We were named 2019 and 2020's #1 fastest-growing independent publisher by *Publishers Weekly*. Our success is driven by our main goal, which is to publish high quality books that will entertain readers as well as make a positive difference in their lives.

Our readers are our most important resource; we value your input, suggestions, and ideas. We'd love to hear from you— after all, we are publishing books for you!

Please stay in touch with us and follow us at:

Facebook: Mango Publishing
Twitter: @MangoPublishing
Instagram: @MangoPublishing
LinkedIn: Mango Publishing
Pinterest: Mango Publishing
Newsletter: mangopublishinggroup.com/newsletter

Join us on Mango's journey to reinvent publishing, one book at a time.

CPSIA information can be obtained
at www.ICGtesting.com
Printed in the USA
LVHW041509161021
700498LV00003B/4